READ ON
BOOK TWO

READ ON

BOOK TWO

DENYS THOMPSON

HEINEMANN

Heinemann Educational Books Ltd
LONDON EDINBURGH MELBOURNE TORONTO
JOHANNESBURG SINGAPORE AUCKLAND
HONG KONG IBADAN NAIROBI

SBN 435 11913 3
Arrangement © Denys Thompson 1969
First Published 1969

Published by
Heinemann Educational Books Ltd
48 Charles Street, London W1X 8AH
Printed in Great Britain by
Butler & Tanner Ltd, Frome and London

FOREWORD

This is the second of five volumes of prose for reading in secondary schools. The self-contained extracts have been enjoyed by a variety of readers, and the series can be used on its own. However, it has wider aims.

First, to encourage readers to explore some of the books from which the extracts are taken, and others like them. Many of the sources from which passages are taken are readily accessible, some in paperback, others in shortened versions. It need hardly be stressed nowadays that reading is the best road to an all-round improvement in English.

Secondly, to provide the core for everything that comes under the heading of English. The pupil's handbook to accompany each volume contains questions leading into every passage, points for discussion, topics for writing and research, and numerous suggestions for related reading, both poetry and prose. A number of the extracts are linked with poems by girls and boys, included both for their own sake and as a stimulus to writing. Finally, for each passage there is a short section on a point of spelling, punctuation, usage or grammar, arising in most cases from the passage itself. These sections are summarised, with other material, at the end of the guide.

D. T.

CONTENTS

4. THIEVES AND DECEIVERS

5. BOYS AND MEN

6. ASSORTED STORIES

ILLUSTRATIONS

BIRD AND BEAST

BADGER

This is a translation of a riddle written in Anglo-Saxon a thousand or more years ago, before the Normans came to England. The handwritten book in which it was recorded was given to Exeter Cathedral (where it still remains) in the time of Edward the Confessor.

My neck is white, my head yellow, also my sides; I am swift in my going, I bear a weapon for battle; on my back stand hairs just as on my cheeks; above my eyes tower two ears; I walk on my toes in the green grass. Grief is doomed for me if anyone, a fierce fighter, catch me in my covert, where I have my haunt, my lair with my litter, and I lurk there with my young brood when the intruder comes to my doors; death is doomed for them, and so I shall bravely bear my children from their abode, save them by flight, if he comes close after me. He goes on his breast; I dare not await his fierceness in my hole – that were ill counsel – but fast with my forefeet I must make a path through the steep hill. I can easily save the life of my precious ones, if I am able to lead my family, my beloved and kin, by a secret way through a hole in the hill; afterwards I need dread not at all the battle with the death-whelp. If the malignant foe pursues me behind by a narrow path, he shall not lack a struggle to bar his way after I reach the top of the hill, and with violence I will strike with war darts the hated enemy whom long I fled.

MISS GOLD SAVES HER CALF

In his Elephant Bill *J. H. Williams tells of his twenty years in Burma, training and caring for the elephants that hauled teak down to the rivers for transport to the saw-mills. Here is one of the many stories he relates of the intelligence of the animals.*

One evening, when the Upper Taungdwin River was in heavy spate, I was listening and hoping to hear the boom and roar of timber coming down from upstream. Directly below my camp the banks of the river were steep and rocky and twelve to fifteen feet high. About fifty yards away on the other side, the bank was made up of ledges of shale strata. Although it was already nearly dusk, by watching these ledges being successively submerged, I was trying to judge how fast the water was rising.

I was suddenly alarmed by hearing an elephant roaring as though frightened, and, looking down, I saw three or four men rushing up and down on the opposite bank in a state of great excitement. I realized at once that something was wrong, and ran down to the edge of the near bank, and there saw Ma Shwe (Miss Gold) with her three-months-old calf, trapped in the fast-rising torrent. She herself was still in her depth, as the water was about six feet deep. But there was a life-and-death struggle going on. Her calf was screaming with terror and was afloat like a cork. Ma Shwe was as near to the far bank as she could get, holding her whole body against the raging and increasing torrent, and keeping the calf pressed against her massive body. Every now and then the swirling water would sweep the calf away; then, with terrific strength, she would encircle it with her trunk and pull it upstream to rest against her body again.

There was a sudden rise in the water, as if a two-foot bore had come down, and the calf was washed clean over the mother's hindquarters and was gone. She turned to chase it, like an otter after a fish, but she had travelled about fifty yards downstream and, plunging and sometimes afloat, had crossed to my side of the river, before she had caught up with it and got it back. For what seemed minutes, she pinned the calf with her head and trunk against the rocky bank. Then, with a really gigantic effort, she picked it up in her trunk and reared up until she was half standing on her hind legs, so as to be able to place it on a narrow shelf of rock, five feet above the flood level.

Having accomplished this, she fell back into the raging torrent, and she herself went away like a cork. She well knew that she would now have a fight to save her own life, as less than 300 yards away below where she had stowed her calf in safety there was a gorge. If she were carried down, it would be certain death. I knew, as well as she did, that there was one spot between her and the gorge where she could get up the bank, but it was on the other side from where she had put her calf. By that time, my chief interest was in the calf. It stood, tucked up, shivering and terrified, on a ledge just wide enough to hold its feet. Its little, fat, protruding belly was tightly pressed against the bank.

While I was peering over at it from about eight feet above, wondering what I could do next, I heard the grandest sounds of a mother's love I can remember. Ma Shwe had crossed the river and got up the bank, and was making her way back as fast as she could, calling the whole time – a defiant roar, but to her calf it was music. The two little ears, like little maps of India, were cocked forward, listening to the only sound that mattered, the call of her mother.

Any wild schemes which had raced through my head of recovering the calf by ropes disappeared as fast as I had formed them, when I saw Ma Shwe emerge from the jungle and appear on the opposite bank. When she saw her calf, she stopped roaring and began rumbling, a never-to-be-forgotten sound, not unlike that made by a very high-powered car when accelerating. It is the sound of pleasure, like a cat's purring, and delighted she must have been to see her calf still in the same spot where she had put her half an hour before.

As darkness fell, the muffled boom of floating logs hitting against each other came from upstream. A torrential rain was falling, and the river still separated the mother and her calf. I decided that I could do nothing but wait and see what happened. Twice before turning in for the night I went down to the bank and picked out the calf with my torch, but this seemed to disturb it, so I went away.

It was just as well I did, because at dawn Ma Shwe and her calf were together – both on the far bank. The spate had subsided to a mere foot of dirty-coloured water. No one in the camp had seen Ma Shwe recover her calf, but she must have lifted it down from the ledge in the same way as she had put it there.

Five years later, when the calf came to be named, the Burmans christened it Ma Yay Yee (Miss Laughing Water).

J. H. Williams (1897–1958), *Elephant Bill*

SQUID

Moby Dick is the story of a great white whale. Ahab seeks to kill him in revenge for an injury he had suffered, and the false alarm described below occurs during the pursuit.

Steering north-eastward from the Crozetts, we fell in with vast meadows of brit, the minute, yellow substance upon which the Right Whale largely feeds. For leagues and leagues it undulated round us, so that we seemed to be sailing through boundless fields of ripe and golden wheat.

On the second day, numbers of Right whales were seen, who, secure from the attack of a sperm-whaler like the *Pequod*, with open jaws sluggishly swam through the brit, which, adhering to the fringing fibres of that wondrous venetian blind in their mouths, was in that manner separated from the water that escaped at the lip.

As morning mowers, who side by side slowly and seethingly advance their scythes through the long wet grass of marshy meads; even so these monsters swam, making a strange, grassy, cutting sound; and leaving behind them endless swaths of blue upon the yellow sea.

Slowly wading through the meadows of brit, the *Pequod* still held on her way north-eastward towards the island of Java. And still, at wide intervals in the silvery night, the lonely, alluring jet would be seen.

But one transparent blue morning, when a stillness apread over the sea; when the slippered waves whispered together as they softly ran on; in this profound hush a strange spectre was seen by Daggoo from the main-masthead.

In the distance, a great white mass lazily rose, and rising higher and higher, and disentangling itself from the azure, at last gleamed before our prow like a snow-slide, new slid from the hills. Thus glistening for a moment, as slowly it subsided, and sank. Then once more arose, and silently sank. It seemed not a

5

whale; and yet is this Moby Dick? thought Daggoo. Again the phantom went down, but on reappearing once more, with a stiletto-like cry that started every man from his nod, the negro yelled out: 'There! there again! there she breaches! right ahead! The white whale, the white whale!'

No sooner did Ahab distinctly perceive the white mass, than with a quick intensity he instantly gave orders for lowering.

The four boats were soon on the water; Ahab's in advance, and all swiftly pulling towards their prey. Soon it went down, and while, with oars suspended, we were awaiting its reappearance, lo! in the same spot where it sank, once more it slowly rose. Almost forgetting for the moment all thoughts of Moby Dick, we now gazed at the most wondrous phenomenon which the secret seas have hitherto revealed to mankind. A vast pulpy mass, furlongs in length and breadth, of a glancing cream colour, lay floating on the water, innumerable long arms radiating from its centre, and curling and twisting like a nest of anacondas, as if blindly to catch at any hapless object within reach. No perceptible face or front did it have; but undulated there on the billows, an unearthly, formless, chance-like apparition of life.

As with a low sucking sound it slowly disappeared again, Starbuck still gazing at the agitated waters where it had sunk, with a wild voice exclaimed: 'Almost rather had I seen Moby Dick and fought him, than to have seen thee, thou white ghost!'

'What was it, sir?' said Flask.

'The great live squid, which, they say, few whale-ships ever beheld, and returned to their ports to tell of it.'

But Ahab said nothing; turning his boat, he sailed back to the vessel; the rest as silently following.

Herman Melville (1819–1891), *Moby Dick* (shortened version by
L. E. C. Bruce)

THE OTTER

Richard Jefferies, the son of a Wiltshire farmer, was born at Swindon. After his first job, on a local newspaper, he became a well-known novelist and writer on the country.

By these rivers of the west, otters are still numerous and are regularly hunted. Besides haunting the rivers, they ascend the brooks, and even the smallest streamlets, and are often killed a long way from the larger waters.

There are three things to be chiefly noticed in the otter – first, the great width of the upper nostril; secondly, the length and sharpness of the hold-fast teeth; and, thirdly, the sturdiness and roundness of the chest or barrel, expressive of singular strength. The upper nostril is so broad that when the mouth is open the lower jaw appears but a third of its width – a mere narrow streak of jaw, dotted, however, with the sharpest teeth. This distension of the upper jaw and narrowness of the lower gives the impression of relentless ferocity. His teeth are somewhat catlike, and so is his manner of biting. He forces his teeth to meet through whatever he takes hold of, but then immediately repeats the bite somewhere else, not holding what he has but snapping again and again like a cat, so that his bite is considered even worse than that of the badger. Now and then, in the excitement of the hunt, a man will put his hand into the hole occupied by the otter to draw him out. If the huntsman sees this there is some hard language, for if the otter chance to catch the hand, he might so crush and mangle it that it would be useless for life. Nothing annoys the huntsman more than interference of this kind.

The otter's short legs are deceptive; it does not look as if a creature so low down could be very serious to encounter or difficult to kill. His short legs are, in fact, an addition to his strength, which is perhaps greater than that of any other animal of proportionate size. He weighs nearly as heavy as a fox, and is even as hard to kill fairly. Unless speared, or knocked heavily on the head, the otter-hounds can rarely kill him in the water; when driven to land at last or to a shallow he is often rather crushed and pressed to death than anything else, and the skin sometimes has not got a single tooth-mark in it. Not a single hound has succeeded in biting through, but there is a different story to tell on the other side. A terrier has his jaw loose and it has to be bound up, such a crushing bite has he had. There are torn shoulders, necks, and limbs, and specks of blood on the nostrils and coats of the other hounds. A full-grown otter fights like a lion in the water; if he gets in a hole under the bank where it is hollow, called a 'hover', he has to be thrust out with a pole. He dives under the path of his enemies as they yelp in the water, and as he goes attacks one from beneath, seizes him by the leg, and drags him down, and almost drowns him before he will let go. The air he is compelled to omit from his lungs as he travels across to another retreat shows his course on the surface, and by the bubbles he is tracked as he goes deep below.

He tries up the stream, and finds at the place where a ledge of rocks crosses it eight or ten men armed with long staves standing waiting for him. If there was but one deep place at the side of the ledge of rocks he could beat them still and slip by, but the water is low for want of rain, and he is unable to do so. He turns and tries at the sides of the river lower down. Behind matted roots, and under the overhanging bank, with a rocky fragment at one side, he faces his pursuers. The hounds are snapped at as they approach in front. He cannot be struck with a staff from above because the bank covers him. Some one must wade across and strike him with a pole till he moves, or carry a terrier or two and pitch them in the hole, half above and half under water. Next he tries the other bank, then baffles all by doubling, till someone spies his nostril as he comes up to breathe. The rocky hill at hand resounds with the cries of the hounds, the sharp bark of the terriers, the orders of the huntsmen, and the shouts of the others. There are ladies in the mead by the river's edge watching the hunt. Met in every direction, the otter swims down stream; there are no rocks there, he knows, but as he comes he finds a net stretched across. He cannot go down the river for the net, nor up it for the guarded ledge of rocks; he is enclosed in a pool without a chance of escape from it, and all he can do is to prolong the unequal contest to the last moment. Now he visits his former holes or 'hovers' to be again found out; now he rests behind rocky fragments, now dives and doubles or eludes all for a minute by some turn. So long as his wind endures or he is not wounded he can stop in the water, and so long as he is in the water he can live. But by degrees he is encircled; some wade in and cut off his course; hounds stop him one way and men the other, till, finally forced to land or to the shallow, he is slain. His webbed feet are cut off and given as trophies to the ladies who are present. The skin varies in colour – sometimes a deep brown, sometimes fawn.

The otter is far wilder than the fox; for the fox a home is found and covers are kept for him, even though he makes free with the pheasants; but the otter has no home except the river and the rocky fastnesses beside it. No creature could be more absolutely wild, depending solely upon his own exertions for existence. Of olden time he was believed to be able to scent the fish in the water at a considerable distance, as a hound scents a fox, and to go straight to them. If he gets among a number he will kill many more than he needs. For this reason he has been driven by degrees from most of the rivers in the south where he used to be found, but still exists in Somerset and Devon. Not even in otter-hunting does he get the same fair play as the fox. No one strikes a fox or puts a net across his course. That, however, is necessary, but it is time that a strong protest was made against the extermination of the otter in rivers like the Thames, where he is treated as a venomous cobra might be on land. The truth is the otter is a most interesting animal and worth preservation, even at the cost of what he eats. There is a great difference between keeping the number of otters down by otter-hunting within reasonable limits and utterly exterminating them. Hunting the otter in Somerset is one thing, exterminating them in the Thames another, and I cannot but feel a sense of deep regret when I hear of fresh efforts towards this end. In the home counties, and, indeed, in many other counties, the list of wild creatures is already short enough, and is gradually decreasing, and the loss of the otter would be serious. The animal is one of the few perfectly wild creatures that have survived without any protection from the ancient forest days. Despite civilization, it still ventures, occasionally, within a few miles of London, and well inside that circle in which London takes its pleasure. It would be imagined that its occurrence so near the metropolis would be recorded with pride; instead of which, no sooner is the existence of an otter suspected than gun and trap are eagerly employed for its destruction.

Richard Jefferies (1848–1887), *The Life of the Fields*

THE PONY EXPRESS

Mark Twain in Roughing It *describes his adventures on his way across America to join his brother in Nevada. Indians and other hazards made the West very wild a hundred years ago, before railways had fully opened up the country.*

In a little while all interest was taken up in stretching our necks and watching for the 'pony-rider' – the fleet messenger who sped across the continent from St. Joe to Sacramento, carrying letters nineteen hundred miles in eight days! Think of that for a perishable horse and human flesh and blood to do! The pony-rider was usually a little bit of a man, brimful of spirit and endurance. No matter what time of the day or night his watch came on, and no matter whether it was winter or summer, raining, snowing, hailing, or sleeting, or whether his 'beat' was a level straight road or a crazy trail over mountain crags and precipices, or whether it led through peaceful regions or regions that swarmed with hostile Indians, he must be always ready to leap into the saddle and be off like the wind! There was no idling-time for a pony-rider on duty. He rode fifty miles without stopping, by daylight, moonlight, starlight, or through the blackness of darkness – just as it happened. He rode a splendid horse that was born for a racer and fed and lodged like a gentleman; kept him at his utmost speed for ten miles, and then, as he came crashing up to the station where stood two men holding fast a fresh, impatient steed, the transfer of rider and mail-bag was made in the twinkling of an eye, and away flew the eager pair, and were out of sight before the spectator could get hardly the ghost of a look. Both rider and horse went 'flying light'. The rider's dress was thin, and fitted close; he wore a 'round-about' and a scull-cap, and tucked his pantaloons into his boot-tops like a race-rider. He carried no arms – he carried nothing that was not absolutely necessary, for even the postage on his literary freight was worth five dollars a letter. He got but little frivolous correspondence to carry – his bag had business letters in it, mostly. His horse was stripped of all unnecessary weight, too. He wore a little wafer of a racing saddle, and no visible blanket. He wore light shoes, or none at all. The little flat mail-pockets strapped under the rider's thighs would each hold about the bulk of a child's primer. They held many and many an important business chapter and newspaper letter, but these were written on paper as airy and thin as gold-leaf, nearly, and thus bulk and weight were economized. The stage-coach travelled about a hundred to a hundred and twenty miles a day (twenty-four hours), the pony-rider about two hundred and fifty. There were about eighty pony riders in the saddle all the time, night and day, stretching in a long, scattering procession from Missouri to California, forty flying eastward, and forty toward the west, and among them making four hundred gallant horses earn a stirring livelihood and see a great deal of scenery every single day in the year.

We had had a consuming desire, from the beginning, to see a pony rider, but somehow or other all that passed us and all that met us managed to streak by in the night, and so we heard only a whiz and a hail, and the swift phantom of the desert was gone before we could get our heads out of the windows. But now we were expecting one along every moment, and would see him in broad daylight. Presently the driver exclaims:
'HERE HE COMES'!
Every neck is stretched farther, and every eye strained wider. Away across the endless dead level of the prairie a black speck appears against the sky, and it is plain that it moves. Well, I should think so! In a second or two it becomes a horse and rider, rising and falling, rising and falling – sweeping toward us nearer and nearer – growing more and more distinct, more and more sharply defined – nearer and still nearer, and the flutter of the hoofs comes faintly to the ear – another instant a whoop and a hurrah from our upper deck, a wave of the rider's hand, but no reply, and man and horse burst past our excited faces, and go winging away like a belated fragment of a storm!

So sudden is it all, and so like a flash of unreal fancy, that but for the flake of white foam left quivering and perishing on a mailsack after the vision had flashed by and disappeared, we might have doubted whether we had seen any actual horse and man at all, maybe.

Mark Twain (1835–1910), *Roughing It*

ADOLF

D. H. Lawrence, the son of a Nottinghamshire miner, was a teacher before he took up full time writing.

When we were children our father often worked on the night-shift. Once it was spring-time, and he used to arrive home, black and tired, just as we were downstairs in our nightdresses. Then night met morning face to face, and the contact was not always happy. Perhaps it was painful to my father to see us gaily entering upon the day into which he dragged himself soiled and weary. He didn't like going to bed in the spring morning sunshine.

But sometimes he was happy, because of his long walk through the dewy fields in the first daybreak. He loved the open morning, the crystal and the space, after a night down pit. He watched every bird, every stir in the trembling grass, answered the whinnying of the peewits and tweeted to the wrens. If he could, he also would have whinnied and tweeted and whistled in a native language that was not human. He liked non-human things best.

One sunny morning we were all sitting at table when we heard his heavy slurring walk up the entry. We became uneasy. His was always a disturbing presence, trammelling. He passed the window darkly, and we heard him go into the scullery and put down his tin bottle. But directly he came into the kitchen. We felt at once that he had something to communicate. No one spoke. We watched his black face for a second.

'Give me a drink,' he said.

My mother hastily poured out his tea. He went to pour it out into his saucer. But instead of drinking he suddenly put something on the table among the teacups. A tiny brown rabbit! A small rabbit, a mere morsel, sitting against the bread as still as if it were a made thing.

'A rabbit! A young one! Who gave it you, father?'

But he laughed enigmatically, with a sliding motion of his yellow-grey eyes, and went to take off his coat. We pounced on the rabbit.

'Is it alive? Can you feel its heart beat?'

My father came back and sat down heavily in his armchair. He dragged his saucer to him, and blew his tea, pushing out his red lips under his black moustache.

'Where did you get it, father?'

'I picked it up,' he said, wiping his naked forearm over his mouth and beard.

'Where?'

'It is a wild one!' came my mother's quick voice.

'Yes, it is.'

'Then why did you bring it?' cried my mother.

'Oh, we wanted it,' came our cry.

'Yes, I've no doubt you did – ' retorted my mother. But she was drowned in our clamour of questions.

On the field path my father had found a dead mother rabbit and three dead little ones – this one alive, but unmoving.

'But what had killed them, daddy?'

'I couldn't say, my child. I s'd think she'd aten something.'

'Why did you bring it!' again my mother's voice of condemnation. 'You know what it will be.'

My father made no answer, but we were loud in protest.

'He must bring it. It's not big enough to live by itself. It would die,' we shouted.

'Yes, and it will die now. And then there'll be *another* outcry.'

My mother set her face against the tragedy of dead pets. Our hearts sank.

'It won't die, father, will it? Why will it? It won't.'

'I s'd think not,' said my father.

'You know well enough it will. Haven't we had it all before!' said my mother.

'They dunna always pine,' replied my father testily.

But my mother reminded him of other little wild animals he had brought, which had sulked and refused to live, and brought storms of tears and trouble in our house of lunatics.

Trouble fell on us. The little rabbit sat on our lap, unmoving, its eye wide and dark. We brought it milk, warm milk, and put it

to its nose. It sat as still as if it was far away, retreated down some
deep burrow, hidden, oblivious. We wetted its mouth and
whiskers with drops of milk. It gave no sign, did not even shake
off the wet white drops. Somebody began to shed a few secret
tears.

'What did I say?' cried my mother. 'Take it and put it down
in the field.'

Her command was in vain. We were driven to get dressed for
school. There sat the rabbit. It was like a tiny obscure cloud.
Watching it, the emotions died out of our breast. Useless to love
it, to yearn over it. Its little feelings were all ambushed. They
must be circumvented. Love and affection were a trespass upon
it. A little wild thing, it became more mute and asphyxiated still
in its own arrest, when we approached with love. We must not
love at. We must circumvent it, for its own existence.

So I passed the order to my sister and my mother. The rabbit
was not to be spoken to, nor even looked at. Wrapping it in a
piece of flannel I put it in an obscure corner of the cold parlour,
and put a saucer of milk before its nose. My mother was forbidden to enter the parlour whilst we were at school.

'As if I should take any notice of your nonsense,' she cried
affronted. Yet I doubt if she ventured into the parlour.

At midday, after school creeping into the front room, there we
saw the rabbit still and unmoving in the piece of flannel. Strange
grey-brown neutralization of life, still living! It was a sore
problem to us.

'Why won't it drink its milk, mother?' we whispered. Our
father was asleep.

'It prefers to sulk its life away, silly little thing.' A profound
problem. Prefers to sulk its life away! We put young dandelion
leaves to its nose. The sphinx was not more oblivious. Yet its eye
was bright.

At tea-time, however it had hopped a few inches out of its
flannel, and there it sat again, uncovered, a little solid cloud of
muteness, brown, with unmoving whiskers. Only its side palpi-
pated slightly with life.

Darkness came; my father set off to work. The rabbit was still
unmoving. Dumb despair was coming over the sisters, a threat
of tears before bedtime. Clouds of my mother's anger gathered
as she muttered against my father's wantonness.

Once more the rabbit was wrapped in the old pit-singlet. But now it was carried into the scullery and put under the copper fireplace, that it might imagine itself inside a burrow. The saucers were placed about, four or five, here and there on the floor, so that if the little creature *should* chance to hop abroad, it could not fail to come upon some food. After this my mother was allowed to take from the scullery what she wanted and then she was forbidden to open the door.

When morning came and it was light, I went downstairs. Opening the scullery door, I heard a slight scuffle. Then I saw dabbles of milk all over the floor and tiny rabbit-droppings in the saucers. And there the miscreant, the tips of his ears showing behind a pair of boots. I peeped at him. He sat bright-eyed and askance, twitching his nose and looking at me while not looking at me.

He was alive – very much alive. But we were still afraid to trespass much on his confidence.

'Father!' My father was arrested at the door. 'Father, the rabbit's alive.'

'Back your life it is,' said my father.

'Mind how you go in.'

By evening, however, the little creature was tame, quite tame. He was christened Adolf. We were enchanted by him. We couldn't really love him, because he was wild and loveless to the end. But he was an unmixed delight.

We decided he was too small to live in a hutch – he must live at large in the house. My mother protested, but in vain. He was so tiny. So we had him upstairs, and dropped his tiny pills on the bed and we were enchanted.

Adolf made himself instantly at home. He had the run of the house, and was perfectly happy, with his tunnels and his holes behind the furniture.

We loved him to take meals with us. He would sit on the table humping his back, hopping off and hobbling back to his saucer, with an air of supreme unconcern. Suddenly he was alert. He hobbled a few tiny paces, and reared himself up inquisitively at the sugar basin. He fluttered his tiny fore-paws, and then reached and laid them on the edge of the basin, whilst he craned his thin neck and peeped in. He trembled his whiskers at the sugar, then did his best to lift down a lump.

'*Do* you think I will have it! Animals in the sugar pot!' cried my mother, with a rap of her hand on the table.

Which so delighted the electric Adolf that he flung his hind-quarters and knocked over a cup.

'It's your own fault, mother. If you left him alone – '

He continued to take tea with us. He rather liked warm tea. And he loved sugar. Having nibbled a lump, he would turn to the butter. There he was shooed off by our parent. He soon learned to treat her shooing with indifference. Still, she hated him to put his nose in the food. And he loved to do it. And one day between them they overturned the cream-jug. Adolf deluged his little chest, bounced back in terror, was seized by his little ears by my mother and bounced down on the hearth-rug. There he shivered in momentary discomfort, and suddenly set off in a wild flight to the parlour.

This last was his happy hunting ground. He had cultivated the bad habit of pensively nibbling certain bits of cloth in the hearth-rug. When chased from this pasture he would retreat under the sofa. There he would twinkle in Buddhist meditation until suddenly, no one knew why, he would go off like an alarm clock. With a sudden bumping scuffle he would whirl out of the room, going through the doorway with his little ears flying. Then we would hear his thunderbolt hurtling in the parlour, but before we could follow, the wild streak of Adolf would flash past us, on an electric wind that swept him round the scullery and carried him back, a little mad thing, flying possessed like a ball round the parlour. After which ebullition he would sit in a corner com-posed and distant, twitching his whiskers in abstract meditation. And it was in vain we questioned him about his outbursts. He just went off like a gun, and was as calm after it as a gun that smokes placidly.

Alas, he grew up rapidly. It was almost impossible to keep him from the outer door.

One day, as we were playing by the stile, I saw his brown shadow loiter across the road and pass into the field that faced the houses. Instantly a cry of 'Adolf!' – a cry that he knew full well. And instantly a wind swept him away down the sloping meadow, his tail twinkling and zigzagging through the grass. After him we pelted. It was a strange sight to see him, ears back, his little loins so powerful, flinging the world behind him. We ran our selves out of breath, but could not catch him. Then some-body headed him off, and he sat with sudden unconcern, twitch-ing his nose under a bunch of nettles.

His wanderings cost him a shock. One Sunday morning my father had just been quarrelling with a pedlar, and we were hearing the aftermath indoors, when there came a sudden unearthly scream from the yard. We flew out. There sat Adolf cowering under a bench, whilst a great black and white cat glowered intently at him, a few yards away. Sight not to be forgotten. Adolf rolling back his eyes and parting his strange muzzle in another scream, the cat stretching forward in a slow elonga-tion.

Ha, how we hated that cat! How we pursued him over the chapel wall and across the neighbours' gardens.

Adolf was still only half grown.

'Cats!' said my mother. 'Hideous detestable animals, why do people harbour them?'

But Adolf was becoming too much for her. He dropped too many pills. And suddenly to hear him clumping downstairs when she was alone in the house was startling. And to keep him from the door was impossible. Cats prowled outside. It was worse than having a child to look after.

Yet we would not have him shut up. He became more lusty, more callous than ever. He was a strong kicker, and many a scratch on face and arms did we owe to him. But he brought his own doom on himself. The lace curtains in the parlour – my mother was rather proud of them – fell on the floor very full. One of Adolf's joys was to scuffle wildly through them as though through some foamy undergrowth. He had already torn rents in them.

One day he entangled himself altogether. He kicked, he whirled round in a mad nebulous inferno. He screamed – and brought down the curtain-rod with a smash, right on the best beloved pelargonium, just as my mother rushed in. She extri-cated him, but she never forgave him. And he never forgave either. A heartless wildness had come over him.

Even we understood that he must go. It was decided, after a long deliberation, that my father should carry him back to the wild-woods. Once again he was stowed into the great pocket of the pit-jacket.

'Best pop him i' th' pot,' said my father, who enjoyed raising the wind of indignation.

And so, next day, our father said that Adolf, set down on the edge of the coppice, had hopped away with utmost indifference, neither elated nor moved. We heard it and believed. But many, many were the heartsearchings. How would the other rabbits receive him? Would they smell his tameness, his humanized degradation, and rend him? My mother pooh-poohed the extravagant idea.

However, he was gone, and we were rather relieved. My father kept an eye open for him. He declared that several times passing the coppice in the early morning, he had seen Adolf peeping through the nettle-stalks. He had called him, in an odd, high-voiced, cajoling fashion. But Adolf had not responded. Wildness gains so soon upon its creatures. And they become so contemptuous then of our tame presence. So it seemed to me. I myself would go to the edge of the coppice, and call softly. I myself would imagine bright eyes between the nettle-stalks, flash of a white, scornful tail past the bracken. That insolent white tail, as Adolf turned his flank on us! It reminded me always of a certain rude gesture . . .

D. H. Lawrence (1885–1930), *Phoenix*

ANIMALS ON BOARD

Captain Slocum rebuilt a 40-ft. sloop, the 'Spray', and set out alone on a voyage round the world that lasted three years. At St. Helena he was given a goat. Other animals were passengers for short spells.

When morning came there was no land in sight, but the day went on the same as days before, save for one small incident. Governor Sterndale had given me a bag of coffee in the husk, and Clark, the American, in an evil moment, had put a goat on board', 'to butt the sack and hustle the coffee-beans out of the pods'. He urged that the animal, besides being useful, would be as companionable as a dog. I soon found that my sailing companion, this sort of dog with horns, had to be tied up entirely. The mistake I made was that I did not chain him to the mast instead of tying him with grass ropes less securely, and this I learned to my cost. Except for the first day, before the beast got his sea-legs on, I had no peace of mind. After that, actuated by a spirit born, maybe, of his pasturage, this incarnation of evil threatened to devour everything from flying-jib to stern-davits. He was the worst pirate I met on the whole voyage. He began depredations by eating my chart of the West Indies, in the cabin, one day, while I was about my work for'ard, thinking that the critter was securely tied on deck by the pumps. Alas! there was not a rope in the sloop proof against the goat's awful teeth!

It was clear from the very first that I was having no luck with animals on board. There was the tree-crab from the Keeling Islands. No sooner had it got a claw through its prison-box than my sea-jacket, hanging within reach, was torn to ribbons. Encouraged by this success, it smashed the box open and escaped into my cabin, tearing up things generally, and finally threatening my life in the dark. I had hoped to bring the creature home alive, but this did not prove feasible. Next the goat devoured my straw hat, and so when I arrived in port I had nothing to wear ashore on my head. This last unkind stroke decided his fate. On the 27th of April the *Spray* arrived at Ascension, which is garrisoned by a man-of-war crew, and the boatswain of the island came on board. As he stepped out of his boat the mutinous goat climbed into it, and defied boatswain and crew. I hired them to land the wretch at once, which they were only too willing to do, and there he fell into the hands of a most excellent Scotchman, with the chances that he would never get away. I was destined to sail once more into the depths of solitude, but these experiences had no bad effect upon me; on the contrary, a spirit of charity and even benevolence grew stronger in my nature through the meditations of these supreme hours on the sea.

In the loneliness of the dreary country about Cape Horn I found myself in no mood to make one life less in the world, except in self-defence, and as I sailed this trait of the hermit character grew till the mention of killing food-animals was revolting to me. However well I may have enjoyed a chicken stew afterward at Samoa, a new self rebelled at the thought suggested there of carrying chickens to be slain for my table on the voyage, and Mrs Stevenson, hearing my protest, agreed with me that to kill the companions of my voyage and eat them would be indeed next to murder and cannibalism.

As to pet animals, there was no room for a noble large dog on the *Spray* on so long a voyage, and a small cur was for many years associated in my mind with hydrophobia. I witnessed once the death of a sterling young German from that dreadful disease, and about the same time heard of the death, also by hydrophobia, of the young gentleman who had just written a line of insurance in his company's books for me. I have seen the whole crew of a ship scamper up the rigging to avoid a dog racing about the decks in a fit. It would never do, I thought, for the crew of the *Spray* to take a canine risk, and with these just prejudices indelibly stamped on my mind, I have, I am afraid, answered impatiently too often the query, 'Didn't you have a dog?' with, 'I and the dog wouldn't have been very long in the same boat, in any sense.' A cat would have been a harmless animal, I dare say, but there was nothing for puss to do on board, and she is an unsociable animal at best. True, a rat got into my vessel at the Keeling Cocos Islands, and another at Rodriguez, along with a centipede stowed away in the hold; but one of them I drove out of the ship and the other I caught. This is how it was: for the first one with infinite pains I made a trap, looking to its capture and destruction; but the wily rodent, not to be deluded, took the hint and got ashore the day the thing was completed.

It is, according to tradition, a most reassuring sign to find rats coming to a ship, and I had a mind to abide the knowing one of Rodriguez; but a breach of discipline decided the matter against him. While I slept one night, my ship sailing on, he undertook to walk over me, beginning at the crown of my head, concerning which I am always sensitive. I slept lightly. Before his impertinence had got him even to my nose I cried 'Rat!', had him by the tail, and threw him out of the companionway into the sea.

As for the centipede, I was not aware of its presence till the wretched insect, all feet and venom, beginning, like the rat, at my head, wakened me by a sharp bite on the scalp. This also was more than I could tolerate. After a few applications of kerosene, the poisonous bite, painful at first, gave me no further inconvenience.

From this on for a time no living thing disturbed my solitude; no insect even was present in my vessel, except the spider and his wife, from Boston, now with a family of young spiders. Nothing, I say, till sailing down the last stretch of the India Ocean, where mosquitoes came by hundreds from rain-water poured out of the heavens. Simply a barrel of rain-water stood on deck five days, I think, in the sun, then music began. I knew the sound at once, it was the same as heard from Alaska to New Orleans.

Again at Cape Town, while dining out one day, I was taken with the song of a cricket, and Mr Branscombe, my host, volunteered to capture a pair of them for me. They were sent on board next day in a box labelled, 'Pluto and Scamp.' Stowing them away in the binnacle in their own snug box, I left them there without food till I got to sea – a few days. I had never heard of a cricket eating anything. It seems that Pluto was a cannibal, for only the wings of poor Scamp were visible when I opened the lid, and they lay broken on the floor of the prison box. Even with Pluto it had gone hard, for he lay on his back stark and stiff, never to chirrup again.

Joshua Slocum (1844–1909), *Sailing Alone Around the World*

THE TYPHLOPS IN DISGUISE

This adventure happened while Gerald Durrell was collecting animals in the Cameroons. ('Na' in pidgin English means roughly 'It is'.)

I had just finished a well-earned cup of tea, and was sitting on the top step in the late sunlight trying to teach an incredibly stupid baby squirrel how to suck milk from a blob of cotton wool on the end of a matchstick. Pausing for a moment in this nerve-racking work, I saw a fat and elderly woman waddling down the road. She was wearing the briefest of loin-cloths, and was smoking a long, slender black pipe. On top of her grey, cropped hair was perched a tiny calabash. When she reached the bottom step, she knocked out her pipe and hung it carefully from the cord round her ample waist, before starting to climb towards the veranda.

'Iseeya, Mammy,' I called.

She stopped and grinned up at me.

'Iseeya, Masa,' she replied, and then continued to heave her body from step to step, panting and wheezing with the exertion. When she reached me, she placed the calabash at my feet, and then leant her bulk against the wall, gasping for breath.

'You done tire, Mammy?' I asked.

'Wah! Masa, I get fat too much,' she explained.

'Fat!' I said in shocked tones; 'you no get fat, Mammy. You no get fat pass me.'

She chuckled richly, and her gigantic body quivered.

'No, Masa, you go fun with me.'

'No, Mammy, I speak true, you be small woman.'

She fell back against the wall, convulsed with laughter at the thought of being called a small woman, her vast stomach and breasts heaving. Presently, when she had recovered from the joke, she gestured at the calabash.

'I done bring beef for you, Masa.'

'Na what kind of beef?'

'Na snake, Masa.'

I unplugged the calabash and peered inside. Coiled up in the bottom was a thin brown snake about eight inches long. I recognized it as a typhlops, a species of blind snake which spends its life burrowing underground. It resembles the English slow-worm in appearance, and is quite harmless. I already had a box full of these reptiles, but I liked my fat girl friend so much that I did not want to disappoint her by refusing it.

'How much you want for dis beef, Mammy?' I asked.

'Eh, Masa go pay me how'e tink.'

'Snake no get wound?'

'No, Masa, atall.'

I turned the calabash upside down and the snake fell out on to the smooth concrete. The woman moved to the other end of the veranda with a speed that was amazing for one so huge.

'E go bite you Masa,' she called warningly.

Jacob, who had appeared to see what was going on, gave the woman a withering look at this remark.

'You no savvay Masa no get fear for dis ting?' he asked. 'Masa get special juju so dis kind of snake no go chop'e.'

'Ah, na so?' said the woman.

I leant forward and picked up the typhlops in my hand, so that I could examine it closely to make sure it was unhurt. I gripped its body gently between my thumb and forefinger, and it twisted itself round my finger. As I looked at it, I noticed a curious thing: it possessed a pair of large and glittering eyes, a thing which no typhlops ever possessed. Foolishly, rather startled by my discovery, I still held the reptile loosely in my hand, and spoke to Jacob.

'Jacob, look, dis snake'e get eye,' I said.

As I spoke, I suddenly realized that I was holding loosely in my hand not a harmless typhlops but some unidentified snake of unknown potentialities. Before I could open my hand and drop it, the snake twisted round smoothly and buried a fang in the ball of my thumb.

Off-hand I can never remember receiving quite such a shock. The bite itself was nothing – like the prick of a pin, followed by a slight burning sensation, rather similar to a wasp sting. I dropped the snake with alacrity, and squeezed my thumb as hard as I could, so that the blood oozed out of the wound, and as I squeezed I

remembered three things. First, there was no snake-bite serum in the Cameroons; secondly, the nearest doctor was some thirty miles away; thirdly, I had no means of getting to him. These thoughts did not make me feel any happier, and I sucked vigorously at the bite, still holding the base of my thumb as tightly as I could. Looking about, I found that Jacob had vanished, and I was just about to utter a roar of rage, when he came scurrying back on to the veranda, carrying in one hand a razor blade, and in the other a couple of ties. Under my frenzied directions, he tied the latter round my wrist and forearm as tightly as he could, and then, with a curious gesture, he handed me the razor blade.

I had never realized before quite how much determination it requires to slash yourself with a razor blade, nor had I realized quite how sharp a razor blade could be. After an awful moment's hesitation, I slashed at my hand, and then found I had given myself a nasty and unnecessary cut about half an inch away from the bite, in a place where it could be of no possible use.

I tried again, with much the same result, and I thought gloomily that if I did not die of the bite, I would probably bleed to death as a result of my own first aid. I thought vindictively of all those books I had read that gave tips on how to deal with snake-bite. All of them, without exception, told you how to make an incision across the bite to the full depth of the fang punctures. It's easy enough to write that sort of thing, but it is quite a different matter to put it into practice successfully when the thumb you are slitting open is your own. There was only one thing to be done, unless I wanted to go on hacking my hand about in the hope of hitting the bite sooner or later. I placed the blade carefully on the ball of my thumb and, gritting my teeth, I pressed and pulled as hard as I could. This was successful, and the blood flowed freely in all directions. The next thing to do, I remembered, was to use permanganate of potash, so I sprinkled some crystals into the gaping wound, and wrapped my hand in a clean handkerchief. By now my hand, wrist, and the glands in my armpit were considerably swollen, and I was getting shooting pains in my thumb, though whether this was due to the bite or to my surgery, I could not tell.

'Masa go for doctor?' asked Jacob, staring at my hand.

'How I go for doctor,' I asked irritably; 'we no get car for dis place. You tink sometimes I go walk?'

2—B

'Masa go ask de Fon for 'e kitcar,' suggested Jacob.

'Kitcar?' I repeated, hope dawning, 'de Fon get kitcar?'

'Yes, sah.'

'Go ask him den . . . one time.'

Jacob galloped down the steps and acrosss the great courtyard, while I paced up and down on the balcony. Suddenly I remembered that in my bedroom reposed a large and un-touched bottle of French brandy, and I sped inside in search of it. I had just managed to pull out the cork when I recalled that all the books on snake-bite were adamant when it came to the point of spirits. On no account, they all stated, must spirits be taken by anyone suffering from snake-bite; apparently they accelerated the heart action and did all sorts of other strange things to you. For a moment I paused, the bottle clutched in one hand; then I decided that if I were going to die I might as well die happy, and I raised the bottle and drank. Warmed and encouraged, I trotted out on to the veranda again, carrying the bottle with me.

A large crowd of people, headed by Jacob and the Fon, were hurrying across the courtyard. They went over to a big hut, and the Fon threw open the door and the crowd poured inside, to reappear almost immediately pushing in front of them an ancient and battered kitcar. They trundled this out through the archway and into the road, and there the Fon left them and hurried up the steps followed by Jacob.

'My friend,' gasped the Fon, 'na bad palaver dis!'

'Na so,' I admitted.

'Your boy done tell me you no get European medicine for dis kind of bite. Na so?'

'Yes, na so. Sometimes doctor done get medicine, I no savvay.'

'By God power 'e go give you medicine,' said the Fon piously.

'You go drink with me?' I asked, waving the bottle of brandy.

'Yes, yes,' said the Fon, brightening, 'we go drink. Drink na good medicine for dis kind of ting.'

Jacob brought glasses and I poured out a liberal measure for us both. Then we went to the top of the steps to see what progress was being made with the preparation of the ambulance.

The kitcar had reposed inside the hut for such a great length of time that its innards seemed to have seized up. Under the driver's gentle ministrations the engine coughed vigorously several times and then ceased. The large crowd round the vehicle clustered closer, all shouting instructions to him, while he leant out of the window and abused them roundly. This went on for some time, and then the driver climbed out and tried to crank her up. This was even less successful, and when he had exhausted himself, he handed the crank to a councillor and went and sat on the running board for a rest. The councillor hitched up his robes and struggled manfully with the crank, but was unable to rouse the engine to life.

The crowd, which now numbered about fifty people, all clamoured for a turn, so the councillor handed the job over to them and joined the driver on the running-board. A disgraceful fight broke out among the crowd as to who would have first turn, and everyone was shouting and pushing and snatching the crank from one another. The uproar attracted the attention of the Fon, and he drained his glass and stalked over to the veranda rail, scowling angrily. He leant over and glared down at the road.

'Wah!' he roared suddenly. 'Start dat motor!'

The crowd fell silent, and all turned to look up at the veranda, while the driver and council members jumped off the running-board and rushed round to the front of the car with an amazing display of enthusiasm. This was somewhat spoilt by the fact that when they did arrive there, the crank was missing. Uproar started again, with everyone accusing everyone else of having lost it. It was found eventually, and the two of them made several more ineffectual attempts to get the engine started.

By now I was beginning to feel rather ill and not at all brave. My hand and forearm had swollen considerably, and were inflamed and painful. I was also getting shooting pains across my shoulders, and my hand felt as though it was grasping a red-hot coal.

It would take me about an hour to reach the doctor, I thought, and if the kitcar did not start soon, there would be little point in going at all. The driver, having nearly ruptured himself in his efforts to crank, was suddenly struck by a brilliant idea. They would push the car. He explained his idea to the crowd, and it was greeted with exclamations of delight and acclamation. The driver got in and the crowd swarmed round behind the kitcar and began to push. Grunting rhythmically, they pushed the kitcar slowly down the road, round the corner and out of sight.

'Soon 'e go start,' smiled the Fon encouragingly, pouring me some more brandy, 'den you go reach doctor one time.'

'You tink 'e go start?' I asked sceptically.

'Yes, yes, ma friend,' said the Fon, looking hurt; 'na my kitcar dis, na foine one. 'E go start small time, no go fear.'

Presently we heard the grunting again, and, on looking over the veranda rail, we saw the kitcar appear round the corner, still being propelled by what seemed to be the entire population of Bafut. It crept towards us like a snail, and then, just as it reached the bottom step, the engine gave a couple of preliminary hiccoughs and then roared into life. The crowd screamed with delight and began to caper about in the road.

"E done start,' explained the Fon proudly, in case I had missed the point of the celebrations.

The driver manœuvred the car through the archway into the courtyard, turned her round, and swept out on to the road again, impatiently tootling his horn and narrowly missing his erstwhile helpers. The Fon and I drained out glasses and then marched down the seventy-five steps. At the bottom the Fon clasped me to his bosom and gazed earnestly into my face. It was obvious that he wanted to say something that would encourage and sustain me on my journey. He thought deeply for a moment.

'My friend,' he said at last, 'if you go die I get sorry too much.'

Not daring to trust my voice, I clasped his hand in what I hoped was a suitably affected manner, climbed into the kitcar and we were off, bouncing and jerking down the road, leaving the Fon and his subjects enveloped in a large cloud of red dust.

Three quarters of an hour later we drew up outside the doctor's house with an impressive squealing of brakes. The doctor was standing outside gloomily surveying a flower-bed. He looked at me in surprise when I appeared, and then, coming forward to greet me, he peered closely into my face.

'What have you been bitten by?' he inquired.

'How did you know I'd been bitten?' I asked, rather startled by this rapid diagnosis.

'Your pupils are tremendously distended,' explained the doctor with professional relish. 'What was it?'

'A snake. I don't know what kind, but it hurts like hell. I don't suppose there was really much use in my coming in to you. There's no serum to be had, is there?'

'Well!' he said in a pleased tone of voice. 'Isn't that a strange thing? Last time I was on leave I got some serum. Thought it might come in useful. It's been sitting in the fridge for the last six months.'

'Well, thank heaven for that.'

'Come into the house, my dear fellow. I shall be most interested to see if it works.'

'So shall I,' I admitted.

We went into the house, and I sat down in a chair while the doctor and his wife busied themselves with methylated spirits, hypodermic needles, and the other accoutrements necessary for the operation. Then the doctor gave me three injections in the thumb, as near to the bite as was possible, and a couple more in my arm. These hurt me considerably more than the original bite had done.

'Made you feel a bit rocky?' inquired the doctor cheerfully, feeling my pulse.

'They've made me feel bloody,' I said bitterly.

'What you need is a good stiff whisky.'

'I thought one wasn't allowed spirits?'

'Oh, yes it won't hurt you,' he said, and poured me out a liberal glassful. I can never remember a drink tasting so good.

'And now,' the doctor went on, 'you're to spend the night in the spare room. I want you in bed in five minutes. You can have a bath if you feel like it.'

'Can't I go back to Bafut?' I asked, 'I've got all my animals there, and there's no one really competent to look after them.'

'You're in no state to go back to Bafut, or to look after animals,' he said firmly. 'Now no arguments, into bed. You can go back in the morning, if I think you're well enough'.

To my surprise I slept soundly, and when I awoke the next day I felt extremely well, though my arm was still swollen and mildly painful. I had breakfast in bed, and then the doctor came to have a look at me.

'How d'you feel?' he asked.

'Fine. I'm feeling so well that I'm beginning to think the snake must have been harmless.'

'No it was poisonous all right. You said it only got you with one fang, and you probably dropped it so quickly that it didn't have time to inject the full shot of venom. If it had, it might have been another story.'

'Can I go back to Bafut?'

'Well, yes, if you feel up to it, but I shouldn't think that arm will be up to much for a day or two. Anyway, if it worries you, come in and see me.'

Spurred on by the thought of my precious collection waiting at Bafut, uncleaned and unfed, I goaded the unfortunate driver so that he got us back in record time. As we drew up in the road below the villa, I saw a figure seated on the bottom step. It was my fat girl friend of the day before.

'Iseeya, Mammy,' I said, as I stepped down into the road.

'Iseeya, Masa,' she replied, hoisting herself to her feet and waddling towards me.

'Na what you de want?' I asked, for I was impatient to get up to my animals.

'Masa done forget?' she inquired, surprised.

'Forget what, Mammy?'

'Eh, Masa!' she said accusingly, 'Masa never pay me for dat fine snake I done bring.'

Gerald Durrell (1925–) *The Bafut Beagles*

2

TIGHT CORNERS

SHADOWED BY WOLVES

Mitchell, the man who met the wolves, was prospecting for gold in Alaska about seventy years ago. He did not find any, but he had many adventures with animals and Indians. He related them to Angus Graham, who made them into a book.

There were two kinds of wolves in the Peel river country, small grey wolves and timber wolves. The grey wolves lived by hunting the caribou in packs of twenty or thirty; in the winter Mitchell used to see them ranging round the herds baying and snapping while the caribou horned them away, keeping the cows and calves inside a kind of hollow square, while big bulls would sometimes charge out from the square and attack the wolves with their fore-feet as well as their horns. But the wolves generally managed to pick out a few weak animals or calves, and were so cunning that they would sometimes drive the caribou over a cliff, where they would break their legs or be killed outright. Grey wolves would only attack a man if he were helpless, and a strong dog could stand up against three or four of them at least. Their method of attack is to slash with their long teeth as they race past, and they prefer not to get to grips, as a dog would do, until the other animal has been thoroughly bewildered and exhausted through loss of blood. But the timber wolves are much more formidable creatures, being so big and strong that two of them can easily pull down a moose. They hunt alone or in couples, and do not bay their prey as the grey wolves do but only call to one another now and then to keep touch as they work through the woods. The Indians used to value their pelts very highly for trade, but even the most skilful Indian hunters found them almost impossible to trap or shoot as their sight and hearing seemed to be supernaturally keen. Sometimes a trapper would get one with a dead-fall set over a kill – they have a habit of returning to their kills after their first feeding – but a dead-fall never succeeds unles fresh snow comes down to cover up the traces of human work, and the trapper must always keep his hands dipped in fresh blood while he is arranging the falls.

This is Mitchell's story of his first encounter with timber wolves.

'I had gone off prospecting by myself, and made a little camp for the night a few miles down-stream from Bear Run Creek. Before I turned in for the night I hung up my gold-pan on a bush – McQuaide had told me that the tinkling of a pan against the branches of a bush would keep me safe from wild animals anywhere. But the next morning, when I went down to the river to fill my billycan, I was horrified to see a dog's tracks that were bigger than my fist. If it was a dog I figured it was too big, and if it was a wolf that wasn't healthy either, so I turned back to my tent, made my breakfast, packed up and got started. But just as I was leaving I saw two prick ears showing up over a brush – it was a wolf all right. The brute shrank down out of sight as I looked, but when I moved on it followed me, keeping under cover, and presently I found that there were two of them, working the hunt together.

'Every now and then one of them showed itself in the open and I had a shot at it, but they were as quick as the devil – you'd think they saw the flash and dodged the bullet, almost – and I never touched them once. After I'd had several cracks at them I happened to look at my belt, and I'd only got two more rounds left! I'd come out with a heavy pack, and had cut down my ammunition to six or eight rounds to save weight. "God," I said, "no more shooting, Mitchell; you keep those rounds for yourself": if they'd got me, I tell you I wasn't going to be torn to pieces alive!

'As I went on without firing the wolves gradually realized that there was no danger, and they got more and more cheeky, keeping closer and closer to me and calling to one another to check up on my movements. They didn't often show themselves out and out, and must have bellied across the open spots like an Indian, but there were always the pointed ears showing over a boulder or a bush, or a flash of grey fur between tree-trunks, and the feeling that you were being watched.

'The worst thing of all was the eyes in the fire-light after dark. I got no sleep that night, as I was keeping up the fire the whole time, and every now and then those eyes would draw up until I had to throw a burning stick at them. All the next day the same thing went on, and no rest again the next night – fire-light, and eyes, and I tell you I was getting pretty rattled. Then on the morning of the third day I saw they'd get me sure if this thing went on, and I thought it was about time to build a raft and go wherever it would take me. So I got hold of some driftwood, strapped it together with my pack-straps and tump-line, and launched myself – and I had to use up one of my two last shots on them as I was pushing off. They followed the raft down along the sands, but eventually it fetched up on the other side of the river, and I got away. Of course the Indians said afterwards that it was my own fault for going out alone.'

After he had finished this story Mitchell suddenly bent forward and banged the arm of his chair. 'Graham,' he said, 'there are no words in the English language that I can use to convey to you the horror of feeling yourself a hunted animal. I shall never forget it – the eyes in the darkness, and the fear of something that lurks. I have been familiar with wolves for years since those days, but I've never got used to the sound of their howling, which is enough to make anyone shudder. Yet those devils that hunted me, they didn't howl – they ran a still-hunt, and that was almost worse in a way. You felt them always pressing on you, always just behind you, always just round that boulder, always watching for the moment when you would stumble or nod asleep – and then leap in!'

Angus Graham, (1892–) *The Golden Grindstone*

LUCKY SURVIVAL

Mark Twain was making his way across America to join his brother in Nevada. This was in the days when the West was indeed wild. After being marooned by floods in an inn, the party set out; they had lost their saddles in the flood.

The next morning it was still snowing furiously when we got away with our new stock of saddles and accoutrements. We mounted and started. The snow lay so deep on the ground that there was no sign of a road perceptible, and the snow-fall was so thick that we could not see more than a hundred yards ahead, else we could have guided our course by the mountain ranges. The case looked dubious, but Ollendorff said his instinct was as sensitive as any compass, and that he could 'strike a bee-line' for Carson City and never diverge from it. He said that if we were to straggle a single point out of the true line his instinct would assail him like an outraged conscience. Consequently we dropped into his wake happy and content. For half an hour we poked along warily enough, but at the end of that time we came upon a fresh trail, and Ollendorff shouted proudly:

'I knew I was as dead certain as a compass, boys! Here we are, right in somebody's tracks that will hunt the way for us without any trouble. Let's hurry up and join company with the party.'

So we put the horses into as much of a trot as the deep snow would allow, and before long it was evident that we were gaining on our predecessors, for the tracks grew more distinct. We hurried along, and at the end of an hour the tracks looked still newer and fresher; but what surprised us was, that the *number* of travellers in advance of us seemed to steadily increase. We wondered how so large a party came to be travelling at such a time and in such a solitude. Somebody suggested that it must be a company of soldiers from the fort, and so we accepted that solution and jogged along a little faster still, for they could not be far off now. But the tracks still multiplied, and we began to think

34

the platoon of soldiers was miraculously expanding into a regiment. Ballou said they had already increased to five hundred! Presently he stopped his horse and said:

'Boys, these are our own tracks, and we've actually been circusing round and round in a circle for more than two hours, out here in this blind desert! By George, this is perfectly hydraulic!'

Then the old man waxed wroth and abusive. He called Ollendorff all manner of hard names – said he never saw such a lurid fool as he was, and ended with the peculiarly venomous opinion that he 'did not know as much as a logarithm!'

We certainly had been following our own tracks. Ollendorff and his 'mental compass' were in disgrace from that moment. After all our hard travel, here we were on the bank of the stream again, with the inn beyond dimly outlined through the driving snow-fall. While we were considering what to do, the young Swede landed from the canoe and took his pedestrian way Carson-wards, singing his same tiresome song about his 'sister and his brother' and 'the child in the grave with its mother,' and in a short minute faded and disappeared in the white oblivion. He was never heard of again. He no doubt got bewildered and lost, and Fatigue delivered him over to Sleep, and Sleep betrayed him to Death. Possibly he followed our treacherous tracks till he became exhausted and dropped.

Presently the Overland stage forded the now fast receding stream and started towards Carson on its first trip since the flood came. We hesitated no longer now, but took up our march in its wake, and trotted merrily along, for we had good confidence in the driver's bump of locality. But our horses were no match for the fresh stage team. We were soon left out of sight; but it was no matter, for we had the deep ruts the wheels made for a guide. By this time it was three in the afternoon, and consequently it was not very long before night came; and not with a lingering twilight, but with a sudden shutting down like a cellar door, as is its habit in that country. The snow-fall was still as thick as ever, and of course we could not see fifteen steps before us; but all about us the white glare of the snow-bed enabled us to discern the smooth sugar-loaf mounds made by the covered sage-bushes, and just in front of us the two faint grooves which we knew were the steadily filling and slowly disappearing wheel-tracks.

Now, those sage-bushes were all about the same height – three

or four feet; they stood just about seven feet apart, all over the
vast desert; each of them was a mere snow-mound now; in *any*
direction that you proceeded (the same as in a well laid out
orchard) you would find yourself moving down a distinctly
defined avenue, with a row of these snow-mounds on either side
of it – an avenue the customary width of a road, nice and level in
its breadth, and rising at the sides in the most natural way, by
reason of the mounds. But we had not thought of this. Then
imagine the chilly thrill that shot through us when it finally
occurred to us, far in the night, that since the last faint trace of the
wheel-tracks had long ago been buried from sight, we might now
be wandering down a mere sage-brush avenue, miles away from
the road, and diverging further and further away from it all the
time. Having a cake of ice slipped down one's back is placid comfort compared to it. There was a sudden leap and stir of blood
that had been asleep for an hour, and as sudden a rousing of all
the drowsing activities in our minds and bodies. We were alive
and awake at once, and shaking and quaking with consternation
too. There was an instant halting and dismounting, a bending
low and an anxious scanning of the road-bed. Useless, of course,
for if a faint depression could not be discerned from an altitude
of four or five feet about it, it certainly could not with one's nose
nearly against it.

We seemed to be in a road, but that was no proof. We tested
this by walking off in various directions – the regular snow-
mounds and the regular avenues between them convinced each
man that *he* had found the true road, and that the others had
found only false ones. Plainly the situation was desperate. We
were cold and stiff, and the horses were tired. We decided to
build a sage-brush fire and camp out till morning. This was wise,
because if we were wandering from the right road and the snow-
storm continued another day, our case would be the next thing
to hopeless if we kept on.

All agreed that a camp fire was what would come nearest to
saving us now, and so we set about building it. We could find no
matches, and so we tried to make shift with the pistols. Not a
man in the party had ever tried to do such a thing before, but not
a man in the party doubted that it *could* be done, and without any
trouble, because every man in the party had read about it in
books many a time, and had naturally come to believe it with

trusting simplicity, just as he had long ago accepted and believed *that other* common book fraud about Indians and lost hunters making a fire by rubbing two dry sticks together.

We huddled together on our knees in the deep snow, and the horses put their noses together and bowed their patient heads over us; and while the feathery flakes eddied down and turned us into a group of white statuary, we proceeded with the momentous experiment. We broke twigs from a sage-bush and piled them on a little cleared place in the shelter of our bodies. In the course of ten or fifteen minutes all was ready, and then, while conversation ceased and our pulses beat low with anxious suspense, Ollendorff applied his revolver, pulled the trigger and blew the pile clear out of the country! It was the flattest failure that ever was.

This was distressing, but it paled before a greater horror – the horses were gone! I had been appointed to hold the bridles, but in my absorbing anxiety over the pistol experiment I had unconsciously dropped them, and the released animals had walked off in the storm. It was useless to try to follow them, for their footfalls could make no sound, and one could pass within two yards of the creatures and never see them. We gave them up without an effort at recovering them, and cursed the lying books that said horses would stay by their masters for protection and companionship in a distressful time like ours.

We were miserable enough before, we felt still more forlorn now. Patiently, but with blighted hope, we broke more sticks and piled them, and once more the Prussian shot them into annihilation. Plainly, to light a fire with a pistol was an art requiring practice and experience, and the middle of a desert at midnight in a snow-storm was not a good place or time for the acquiring of the accomplishment. We gave it up and tried the other. Each man took a couple of sticks and fell to chafing them together. At the end of half an hour we were thoroughly chilled, and so were the sticks. We bitterly execrated the Indians, the hunters, and the books that had betrayed us with the silly device, and wondered dismally what was next to be done. At this critical moment Mr Ballou fished out four matches from the rubbish of an overlooked pocket. To have found four gold bars would have seemed poor and cheap good luck compared to this. One cannot think how good a match looks under such circumstances – or how loveable and precious, and sacredly beautiful to the eye. This time we gathered sticks with high hopes; and when Mr Ballou prepared to light the first match, there was an amount of interest centred upon him that pages of writing could not describe. The match burned hopefully a moment, and then went out. It could not have carried more regret with it if it had been a human life. The next match simply flashed and died. The wind puffed the third one out just as it was on the imminent verge of success. We gathered together closer than ever, and developed a solicitude that was rapt and painful, as Mr Ballou scratched our last hope on his leg. It lit, burned blue and sickly, and then budded into a robust flame. Shading it with his hands, the old gentleman bent gradually down, and every heart went with him – every body too, for that matter – and blood and breath stood still. The flame touched the sticks at last, took gradual hold upon them, hesitated, took a stronger hold, hesitated again, held its breath five heart-breaking seconds, then gave a sort of human gasp and went out.

Nobody said a word for several minutes. It was a solemn sort of silence; even the wind put on a stealthy, sinister quiet, and made no more noise than the falling flakes of snow. Finally a sad-voiced conversation began, and it was soon apparent that in each of our hearts lay the conviction that this was our last night with the living. I had so hoped that I was the only one who felt so. When the others calmly acknowledged their conviction, it sounded like the summons itself. Ollendorff said:

'Brothers, let us die together. And let us go without one hard feeling towards each other. Let us forget and forgive bygones. I know that you have felt hard towards me for turning over the canoe, and for knowing too much and leading you round and round in the snow; but I meant well: forgive me. I acknowledge freely that I have had hard feelings against Mr Ballou for abusing me and calling me a logarithm, which is a thing I do not know what, but no doubt a thing considered disgraceful and unbecoming in America, and it has scarcely been out of my mind, and has hurt me a great deal; but let it go; I forgive Mr Ballou with all my heart, and –'

Poor Ollendorff broke down, and the tears came. He was not alone, for I was crying too, and so was Mr Ballou. Ollendorff got his voice again, and forgave me for things I had done and said. Then he got out his bottle of whisky and said that whether he lived or died he would never touch another drop. He said he had given up all hope of life, and although ill prepared, was ready to submit humbly to his fate; that he wished he could be spared a little longer, not for any selfish reason, but to make a thorough reform in his character, and by devoting himself to helping the poor, nursing the sick, and pleading with the people to guard themselves against the evils of intemperance, make his life a beneficent example to the young, and lay it down at last with the previous reflection that it had not been lived in vain. He ended by saying that his reform should begin at this moment, even here in the presence of death, since no longer time was to be vouchsafed wherein to prosecute it to men's help and benefit – and with that he threw away the bottle of whisky.

Mr Ballou made remarks of similar purport, and began the reform he could not live to continue, by throwing away the ancient pack of cards that had solaced our captivity during the flood and made it bearable. He said he never gambled, but still was satisfied that the meddling with cards in any way was im-moral and injurious, and no man could be wholly pure and blemishless without eschewing them. 'And therefore,' continued he, 'in doing this act I already feel more in sympathy with that spiritual saturnalia necessary to entire and obsolete reform.' These rolling syllables touched him as no intelligible eloquence could have done, and the old man sobbed with a mournfulness not unmingled with satisfaction.

My own remarks were of the same tenor as those of my com-rades, and I know that the feelings that prompted them were heartfelt and sincere. We were all sincere, and all deeply moved and earnest, for we were in the presence of death and without hope. I threw away my pipe, and in doing it felt that at last I was free of a hated vice, and one that had ridden me like a tyrant all my days. While I yet talked, the thought of the good I might have done in the world and the still greater good I might *now* do, with these new incentives and higher and better aims to guide me if I could only be spared a few years longer, overcame me, and the tears came again. We put our arms about each other's necks and awaited the warning drowsiness that precedes death by freezing.

It came stealing over us presently, and then we bade each other a last farewell. A delicious dreaminess wrought its web about my yielding senses, while the snow-flakes wove a winding-sheet about my conquered body. Oblivion came. The battle of life was done.

I do not know how long I was in a state of forgetfulness, but it seemed an age. A vague consciousness grew upon me by degrees, and then came a gathering anguish of pain in my limbs and through all my body. I shuddered. The thought flitted through my brain, 'this is death – this is the hereafter.'

Then came a white upheaval at my side, and a voice said, with bitterness,

'Will some gentleman be so good as to kick me behind?'

It was Ballou – at least, it was a towzled snow image in a sitting posture, with Ballou's voice.

I rose up, and there in the grey dawn, not fifteen steps from us, were the frame buildings of a stage station, and under a shed stood our still saddled and bridled horses!

I have scarcely exaggerated a detail of this curious and absurd adventure. It occurred almost exactly as I have stated it. We actually went into camp in a snowdrift in a desert, at midnight in a storm, forlorn and hopeless, within fifteen steps of a comfortable inn.

Mark Twain (1835–1910), *Roughing It*

THE CROSSING

*John Bunyan was a tinker who suffered many years' imprison-
ment for refusing to conform to the official religion of the seventeenth
century. During one prison spell he started* The Pilgrim's Progress
*– the story of Christian's journey through life. This passage comes
from the end of the second book.*

When days had many of them passed away, Mr Despondency
was sent for; for a post was come, and brought this message to
him: Trembling man, these are to summon thee to be ready with
thy King by the next Lord's day, to shout for joy for thy deliver-
ance from all thy doubtings. Now, Mr Despondency's daughter,
whose name was Much-afraid, said, when she heard what was
done, that she would go with her father.

When the time was come for them to depart, they went to the
brink of the river. The last words of Mr Despondency were,
Farewell night, welcome day. His daughter went through the
river singing, but none could understand what she said.

Then it came to pass, a while after, that there was a post in the
town that inquired for Mr Honest. So he came to his house where
he was, and delivered to his hand these lines: Thou art commanded to be ready against this day seven-night, to present thyself before thy Lord, at his Father's house. And for a token that
my message is true, 'All thy daughters of music shall be brought
low.' Then Mr Honest called for his friends, and said unto them,
I die, but shall make no will. As for my honesty, it shall go with
me; let him that comes after be told of this. When the day that
he was to be gone was come, he addressed himself to go over the
river. Now the river at that time overflowed the banks in some
places; but Mr Honest in his lifetime had spoken to one Good-
conscience to meet him there, the which he also did, and lent
him his hand, and so helped him over. The last words of Mr
Honest were, Grace reigns. So he left the world.

After this it was noised abroad, that Mr Valiant-for-truth was
taken with a summons by the same post as the other; and had

this for a token that the summons was true, 'That his pitcher was broken at the fountain.' When he understood it, he called for his friends, and told them of it. Then, said he, I am going to my Father's; and though with great difficulty I am got hither, yet now I do not repent me of all the trouble I have been at to arrive where I am. My sword I give to him that shall succeed me in my pilgrimage, and my courage and skill to him that can get it. My marks and scars I carry with me, to be a witness for me, that I have fought his battles who now will be my rewarder. When the day that he must go hence was come, many accompanied him to the riverside, into which as he went he said, 'Death, where is thy sting?' And as he went down deeper, he said, 'Grave, where is thy victory?' So he passed over, and all the trumpets sounded for him on the other side.

Then there came forth a summons for Mr Stand-fast – this Mr Stand-fast was he that the rest of the pilgrims found upon his knees in the Enchanted Ground – for the post brought it him open in his hands. The contents whereof were, that he must prepare for a change of life, for his Master was not willing that he should be so far from him any longer. At this Mr Stand-fast was put into a muse. Nay, said the messenger, you need not doubt the truth of my message, for here is a token of the truth thereof: 'Thy wheel is broken at the cistern.' Then he called unto him Mr Great-heart, who was their guide, and said unto him, Sir, although it was not my hap to be much in your good company in the days of my pilgrimage; yet, since the time I knew you, you have been profitable to me. When I came from home, I left behind me a wife and five small children; let me entreat you, at your return (for I know that you will go and return to your Master's house, in hopes that you may yet be a conductor to more of the holy pilgrims), that you send to my family, and let them be acquainted with all that hath or shall happen unto me. Tell them, moreover, of my happy arrival to this place, and of the present (and) late blessed condition that I am in. Tell them also of Christian, and Christiana his wife, and how she and her children came after her husband. Tell them also of what a happy end she made, and whither she has gone. I have little or nothing to send to my family, except it be prayers and tears for them; of which it will suffice if thou acquaint them, if peradventure they may prevail.

When Mr Stand-fast had thus set things in order, and the time being come for him to haste him away, he also went down to the river. Now there was a great calm at that time in the river; wherefore Mr Stand-fast, when he was about half-way in, stood awhile, and talked to his companions that had waited upon him thither; and he said, This river has been a terror to many; yea, the thoughts of it also have often frightened me. Now, methinks, I stand easy, my foot is fixed upon that upon which the feet of the priests that bare the ark of the covenant stood, while Israel went over this Jordan. The waters, indeed, are to the palate bitter, and to the stomach cold; yet the thoughts of what I am going to, and of the conduct that waits for me on the other side, doth lie as a glowing coal at my heart.

I see myself now at the end of my journey, my toilsome days are ended. I am going now to see that head that was crowned with thorns, and that face that was spit upon for me.

I have formerly lived by hearsay and faith; but now I go where I shall live by sight, and shall be with him in whose company I delight myself.

I have loved to hear my Lord spoken of; and wherever I have seen the print of his shoe in the earth, there I have coveted to set my foot too.

His name has been to me as a civet-box; yea, sweeter than all perfumes. His voice to me has been most sweet; and his countenance I have more desired than they that have most desired the light of the sun. His word I did use to gather for my food, and for antidotes against my faintings. 'He has held me, and hath kept me from mine iniquities; yea, my steps hath he strengthened in his way.'

Now, while he was thus in discourse, his countenance changed, his strong man bowed under him; and after he had said, Take me, for I come unto thee, he ceased to be seen of them.

But glorious it was to see how the open region was filled with horses and chariots, with trumpeters and pipers, with singers and players on stringed instruments, to welcome the pilgrims as they went up, and followed one another in at the beautiful gate of the city.

John Bunyan (1628–1688), *The Pilgrim's Progress*

THE DELUGE

At Christmas and Easter in the Middle Ages one of the chief entertainments in the towns were the mystery plays. These were dramatic versions of the main events recorded in the Bible. Usually there was a key copy kept by the local authorities, who every year distributed the production of the plays among the various guilds. They were then performed on wagons in different parts of the town over several days. The play that follows is one of a sequence of twenty-four plays performed at Chester; the 'Waterleaders and Drawers in the Dee' were responsible for staging it.

NOAH'S DELUGE

God: I, God, that all the world have wrought:
Heaven and earth and all from naught,
I see my people in deed and thought
Are set foully in sin.

My joy cannot linger in man
That, through sin, lies under my ban.
But wait six score years more I can
To leave their old sin.

Man that I made I will destroy,
Beast, worm and fowl all die,
For on earth all me deny,
Those folk that dwell thereon.

It harms me so hurtfully,
That malice should multiply.
Sore it pains me inwardly,
That ever I made man.

Therefore, Noah, my servant free,
That righteous man art as I can see,
A ship soon thou shalt make thee
Of trees dry and light.

Little chambers therein thou shalt make
And binding ropes also thou take.
Cease not with cord and with stake
To make fast with all thy might.

Three hundred cubits shall it be long
And Fifty in breadth to make it strong,
Fifty more high, so be ye not wrong
And measure it about.

One window make with thy might
One cubit in breadth and height.
In the side a door fit thou right
For to come in and out.

Eating places make thou also,
High roofed chambers, one or two,
For with water I mean to flow
Over that man I did make.

Destroyed all the world shall be
Save thou, thy wife, and sons three,
And all their wives also with thee
Shall be saved for thy sake.

Noah: Ah, lord, I thank thee loud and still
That to me art in good will,
And spare me and my home not spill
As here now I find.

Thy bidding, Lord, I shall fulfil,
And never shall grieve or do ill
That such grace shows your high will
Among all mankind.

Have done, you men and women all,
Help in whatever may now befall
To work this ship, build chamber and hall
As God has bidden us do.

Shem: Father, here I am come from the town
An axe I have here, by my crown.
I lay we shall not soon drown.
Let us go to.

Ham: I have a hatchet wondrous keen,
To bite well as may be seen,
One better ground, sure I ween,
Is not in this town.

Japhet: And I can make such a pin
And with this hammer knock it in.
Go and work without more din
Then we shall not drown.

Mother Noah: And we shall bring timber to you.
There is nothing else that we can do
For women are weak yet they will help too
In this great travail.

Shem's Wife: Here is a good hackstock:
On this you may hew and knock.
There shall none be idle in all this flock
And no one shall fail.

Ham's Wife: And I will go and heat some pitch
To daub and fill up every niche.
Anointed it must be in every stitch,
Board, tree and pin.

Japhet's Wife: And I will gather woodchips here
To make a fire for you, for fear
There is no meal done here
Against your coming in.

Noah: Now in the name of God I will begin
To make the ship we shall go in
That we may all be ready to swim
At the coming of the flood.

These boards I join here together
To keep us safe in the wet weather
That we may row hither and thither
And be safe from the flood.

Of this tree will I make the mast
Tied up with cables that will last
With a sail yard for every sharp blast
And whatever God send.

With topsail and bowsprit
With cords and ropes I have what is fit
To sail forth when it grows wet.
This ship is at an end.

Wife, in this castle we shall be kept,
When my children and you in have leapt.

Mother Noah: In faith, Noah, I would sooner you slept
Than all this stupid fussing.
I will not do as you have said.

Noah: Good wife, do as I thee bid.

Mother Noah: By Christ! not till I see more need
Though you stand all day here staring.

Noah: Lord, all women are crabbed. Aye!
And never are meek, that I will say.
This is well seen on earth this day
Which witness you, each one.

Good wife, let be all this jeer
That thou makest standing here,
For all will think you are master
And so thou art, by St. John.

God: Noah, take now thy family
And into the ship with thee,
For none so righteous to me
Is now on earth living.

Of clean beasts with thee thou must take
Seven and seven, for my sake,
He and she, mates to make,
These are what you must bring.

Of beasts unclean two and two,
Male and female, in counting be true.
Of clean fowls seven bring through
Then, he and she together.

Of fowls unclean two and no more
As of the beasts I said just before.
These shall be saved from dangers sore
When I send the bad weather.

Of all the meats that must be eaten
Now into the hold see they be gotten;
For that must not at all be forgotten.
And do this full soon.

To sustain man and beast withal
Until the waters shall cease and fall.
This world is sinful in all
As I see each noon.

Seven days are yet coming
For you to gather and bring
Those after my liking
When mankind I annoy.

Forty days and forty nights
Rain shall fall for their unrights
And those I have made through my mights
Now I think to destroy.

Noah: Lord, at your bidding I am true
Since grace is only in you,
As you ask I will do.
For gracious I you find.

One hundred winters and twenty
This ship making, tarried have I
Lest through amendment any mercy
Should fall to mankind.

Have done, you men and women all
Hurry lest the waters fall,
See each beast fast into his stall
And safe in our ship brought.

Of clean beasts seven shall be;
Of unclean two, as God bade me;
The flood is high, as ye may well see,
Therefore tarry you naught.

(The family and animals enter the ark)

Shem: Sir, here are lions, leopards in,
Horses, mares, ox and swine,
Goats, calves, sheep and kine
Here sitting thou mayst see.

Ham: Camels, asses, men many find,
Buck, doe, hart and hind,
And beasts of all other kind
Are here, it seems to me.

Japhet: Look here cats and dogs all go,
Otter, fox, fulmart also,
Hares hopping gaily on toe
Have plenty here to eat.

Mother Noah: And here are bears, and wolves a set,
Apes, owls and marmoset,
Weasels, squirrels and ferret,
Here they have eaten their meat.

Shem's Wife: Yet more beasts are in this house.
Here are cats who all carouse
Here are rats and there a mouse.
Lo! they stay close together.

Ham's Wife: And here are greater and lesser fowls,
Herons, cranes, bitterns, owls,
Swans, peacocks, and in those bowls
Food for this weather.

Japhet's Wife: Here are cocks, kites, crows,
Rooks, ravens, and many rows
Of ducks, curlews, whoever knows
Each one in his kind?

And here come doves, ducks, drakes,
Redshanks running up from the lakes;
For every fowl that birdsong makes
In this ship we can find.

Noah: Wife, come! why standest there?
Thou art always froward, that I dare swear.
Now come, a God's name, time it were
For fear lest we drown.

Mother Noah: Yea, Sir, set up your sail
And row forth, so hearty and hale,
For, without any fail,
I will not out of our town.

For I have my gossips everyone.
One foot further I will not be gone
For they shall not drown, by St John,
If I may save their life.

They love me full well, by Christ,
Though thou wilt not let them in this chest,
So you row forth, Noah, when you list
And get thee a new wife.

Noah: Shem, son, thy mother is raw, lo,
In truth such a trouble I do not know.

Shem: Father, I will fetch her in, I trow,
Without any fail.

Mother, my father after thee does send
To bid thee upon the ship to wend.
Look up and see the wind.
We are ready to sail.

Mother Noah: Son, go back to him and say
I will not step inside today.

Noah: Come in wife! Oh, your devilish way!
Or else stay there without.

Ham: Shall we fetch her in ?

Noah: Yes, sons, with Christ's blessing and mine:
For here comes of the rain a first sign,
And of this flood I am in no doubt.

Japhet: Mother, we pray you altogether
Since we are here your own childer,
Come into the ship for fear of the weather
For his love that you has bought.

Mother Noah: That will I not for all your call
Unless I have my gossips all.

Shem: In faith, mother, yet you shall,
Whether you will or not.

(Forces her in)

Noah: Welcome at last into our boat.

Mother Noah: Now take that to thy note.

(*Boxes his ears*)

Noah: Ha! marry, this is too hot,
It is good to be still!

Ah! children, me thinks the boat doth give;
Tarrying here me much doth grieve
While over the land the waters do spread
God does as he will!

Ah! great God that art so good.
He that does not thy will is but a clod.
Now all the world is in a flood
As I see well in sight.

This window I will shut anon
And into my chamber now be gone
Till this water, Most Great One,
Slacks off through thy might.

(*Closes window. Sings from Psalm* 79)

Now forty days are fully gone
Send I a raven will anon:
If anywhere, earth, tree or stone
Is dry in any place.

(*Opens window*)

And if this bird come not again,
It is a sign, I maintain,
That it is dry on hill or plain
And God has sent his grace.

(*Raven sent out*)

Ah, Lord, wherever this raven be
That place is dry, well we see;
But now a dove, by my loyalty,
After her will I send.

(*Dove despatched*)

Ah, Lord, blessed be thou aye,
That hast given us comfort here today!
For now I truly can say
This flood begins to cease.

My sweet dove has brought apace
A branch of olive from some place
Which proves that God has shown us grace
And is a sign of peace.

Ah, Lord, honoured must thou be,
All earth dries now I can see,
But till thou commandest to me
Hence I will not hie.

All the water is away
Therefore as soon as I may
Sacrifice I shall this day
To thee devoutly.

God: Noah, take thy wife anon,
And thy children every one;
Out of the ship thou shalt be gone
And all with thee.

Beasts and all that can fly
Out from here may hie
To earth to grow and multiply
I will that it be so.

Noah: Lord, I thank thee for thy might.
Thy bidding shall be done in the height.
For thy mercies, Lord, as is right.
I will do thee honour.

For to offer thee sacrifice
Come all in this manner wise,
For of the beasts that are his
I offer back this store.

(*Offerings made on altar*)

God: Noah, to me thou art full able
And thy sacrifice acceptable;
For I know thee to be true and stable,
Of thee must I be mindful.

Worry earth, I will no more
Though man's sin grieves me still sore
And the youthful as of yore
Are always found sinful.

You shall now grow and multiply
The earth again shall edify
And beast and fowl that fly
Shall live in fear of you.

And fish swimming in the sea
Shall feed you, believe you me,
To eat all these you are quite free
They are clean as you may know.

My Bow between you and me
In the firmament shall be
As a true token for all to see
That this vengeance shall cease.

That man and woman shall never more
Be devastated by water as before.
For sin that grieveth me sore
Remember the vengeance was.

Where clouds in the skies have been
That new bow shall be seen
In token that my wrath and spleen
Never again shall wreakèd be.

The string is turned towards you
And towards me is bent the bow
That such weather shall never show,
And this promise I thee.

My blessing now I give thee here
To thee, Noah, my servant dear.
For vengeance shall no more appear.
And now fare well, my darling dear.

HURRICANE

F. T. Bullen was born of Somerset parents over a hundred years ago. He attended school only till he was nine. After that he was a street-arab in London, till at twelve he went to sea. This comes from his story of a voyage in an American whaler.

The wind blew fitfully in short gusts, veering continually back and forth over about a quarter of the compass. Although it was still light, it kept up an incessant mournful moan not to be accounted for in any way. Darker and darker grew the heavens, although no clouds were visible, only a general pall of darkness. Glimmering lightnings played continually about the eastern horizon, but not brilliant enough to show us the approaching storm-cloud. And so came the morning of the third day from the beginning of the change. But for the clock we should hardly have known that day had broken, so gloomy and dark was the sky. At last light came in the east, but such a light as no one would wish to see. It was a lurid glare, much as may be seen playing over a cupola of Bessemer steel when the spiegeleisen is added, only on such an extensive scale that its brilliancy was dulled into horror. Then, beneath it we saw the mountainous clouds fringed with dull violet and with jagged sabres of lightning darting from their solid black bosoms. The wind began to rise steadily but rapidly, so that by eight a.m. it was blowing a furious gale from ENE. In direction it was still unsteady, the ship coming up and falling off to it several points. Now, great masses of torn, ragged cloud hurtled past us above, so low down as almost to touch the mastheads. Still the wind increased, still the sea rose, till at last the skipper judged it well to haul down the tiny triangle of storm stay-sail still set (the topsail and fore stay-sail had been furled long before), and let her drift under bare poles, except for three square feet of stout canvas in the weather mizen-rigging. The roar of the wind now dominated every sound, so that it might have been thundering furiously, but we should not have heard it.

The ship still maintained her splendid character as a sea-boat, hardly shipping a drop of water; but she lay over at a most distressing angle, her deck sloping off fully thirty-five to forty degrees. Fortunately she did not roll to windward. It may have been raining in perfect torrents, but the tempest tore off the surface of the sea, and sent it in massive sheets continually flying over us, so that we could not possibly have distinguished between fresh water and salt.

The chief anxiety was for the safety of the boats. Early on the second day of warning they had been hoisted to the top-most notch of the cranes, and secured as thoroughly as experience could suggest; but at every lee lurch we gave it seemed as if we must dip them under water, while the wind threatened to stave the weather ones in by its actual solid weight. It was now blowing a furious cyclone, the force of which has never been accurately gauged (even by the present elaborate instruments of various kinds in use). That force is, however, not to be imagined by any one who has not witnessed it, except that one notable instance is on record by which mathematicians may get an approximate estimate.

Captain Toynbee, the late highly respected and admired Marine Superintendent of the British Meteorological Office, has told us how, during a cyclone which he rode out in the *Hotspur* at Sandheads, the mouth of the Hoogly, the three naked topgallant-masts of his ship, though of well-tested timber a foot in diameter, and supported by all the usual network of stays, and without the yards, were snapped off and carried away solely by the violence of the wind. It must, of course, have been an extreme gust, which did not last many seconds, for no cable that was ever forged would have held the ship against such a cataclysm as that. This gentleman's integrity is above suspicion, so that no exaggeration could be charged against him, and he had the additional testimony of his officers and men to this otherwise incredible fact.

The terrible day wore on, without any lightening of the tempest, till noon, when the wind suddenly fell to a calm. Until that time, the sea, although heavy, was not vicious or irregular, and we had not shipped any heavy water at all. But when the force of the wind was suddenly withdrawn, such a sea rose as I have never seen before or since. Inky mountains of water raised their savage heads in wildest confusion, smashing one another in whirlpools of foam. It was like a picture of the primeval deep out of which arose the newborn world. Suddenly out of the whirling blackness overhead the moon appeared, nearly in the zenith, sending down through the apex of a dome of torn and madly gyrating cloud a flood of brilliant light. Illumined by that startling radiance, our staunch and seaworthy ship was tossed and twirled in the hideous vortex of mad sea until her motion was distracting. It was quite impossible to loose one's hold and attempt to do anything without running the imminent risk of being dashed to pieces. Our decks were full of water now, for it tumbled on board at all points; but as yet no serious weight of a sea had fallen upon us, nor had any damage been done. Such a miracle as that could not be expected to continue for long. Suddenly a warning shout rang out from somewhere – 'Hold on all, for your lives!' Out of the hideous turmoil around arose, like some black, fantastic ruin, an awful heap of water. Higher and higher it towered, until it was level with our lower yards, then it broke and fell upon us. All was blank. Beneath that mass every thought, every feeling, fled but one – 'How long shall I be able to hold my breath?' After what seemed a never-ending time, we emerged from the wave more dead than alive, but with the good ship still staunch underneath us, and Hope's lamp burning brightly. The moon had been momentarily obscured, but now shone out again, lighting up brilliantly our bravely-battling ship. But, alas for others! – men, like ourselves, whose hopes were gone. Quite near us was the battered remainder of what had been a splendid ship. Her masts were gone, not even the stumps being visible, and it seemed to our eager eyes as if she was settling down. It was even so, for as we looked, unmindful of our own danger, she quietly disappeared – swallowed up with her human freight in a moment, like a pebble dropped into a pond.

While we looked with hardly beating hearts at the place where she had sunk, all was blotted out in thick darkness again. With a roar, as of a thousand thunders, the tempest came once more, but from the opposite direction now. As we were under no sail, we ran little risk of being caught aback; but, even had we, nothing could have been done, the vessel being utterly out of control, besides the impossibility of getting about. It so happened, however, that when the storm burst upon us again, we were stern on to it, and we drove steadily for a few moments until we had time to haul to the wind again. Great heavens! how it blew! Surely, I thought, this cannot last long – just as we sometimes say of the rain when it is extra heavy. It did last, however, for what seemed an interminable time, although any one could see that the sky was getting kindlier. Gradually, imperceptibly, it took off, the sky cleared, and the tumult ceased, until a new day broke in untellable beauty over a revivified world.

Years afterwards I read, in one of the hand-books treating of hurricanes and cyclones, that 'in the centre of these revolving storms the sea is so violent that few ships can pass through it and live.' That is true talk. I have been there, and bear witness that but for the build and sea-kindliness of the *Cachalot* she could not have come out of that horrible cauldron again, but would have joined that nameless unfortunate whom we saw succumb, 'never again heard of.' As it was, we found two of the boats stove in, whether by breaking sea or crushing wind nobody knows. Most of the planking of the bulwarks was also gone, burst outward by the weight of the water on deck. Only the normal quantity of water was found in the well on sounding, and not even a rope-yarn was gone from aloft. Altogether, we came out of the ordeal triumphantly, where many a gallant vessel met her fate, and the behaviour of the grand old tub gave me a positive affection for her, such as I have never felt for a ship before or since.

F. T. Bullen (1857–1915), *The Cruise of the 'Cachalot'*

THE TERROR OF STAMPEDE

Jock was a dog whose master sought gold in South Africa. The search failed, and the two joined a group of four wagons. While on trek the men lived by hunting, and the book consists mainly of hunting episodes. While pursuing a wounded buffalo, the party is checked by a fire lit by native Africans.

They habitually fire the grass in patches during the summer and autumn, as soon as it is dry enough to burn, in order to get young grass for the winter or the early spring, and although the smoke worried us there did not seem to be anything unusual about the fire. But ten minutes later we stopped again; the smoke was perceptibly thicker; birds were flying past us down wind, with numbers of locusts and other insects; two or three times we heard buck and other animals break back; and all were going the same way. Then the same thought struck us both – it was stamped in our faces: this was no ordinary mountain grass fire; it was the bush.

Francis was a quiet fellow, one of the sort it is well not to rouse. His grave is in the Bushveld where his unbeaten record among intrepid lion-hunters was made, and where he fell in the war, leaving another and greater record to his name. The blood rose slowly to his face, until it was bricky red, and he looked an ugly customer as he said:

'The blacks have fired the valley to burn him out. Come on quick. We must get out of this on to the slopes!'

We did not know then that there were no slopes – only a precipitous face of rock with dense jungle to the foot of it; and after we had spent a quarter of an hour in that effort, we found our way blocked by the krans and a tangle of undergrowth much worse than that in the middle of the terrace. The noise made by the wind in the trees and our struggling through the grass and bush had prevented our hearing the fire at first, but now its ever growing roar drowned all sounds. Ordinarily, there would have

60

been no real difficulty in avoiding a bush fire; but, pinned in between the river and the precipice and with miles of dense bush behind us, it was not at all pleasant.

Had we turned back even then and made for the poort it is possible we might have travelled faster than the fire, but it would have been rough work indeed; moreover, that would have been going back – and we did want to get the buffalo – so we decided to make one more try, towards the river this time. It was not much of a try, however, and we had gone no further than the middle of the terrace again when it became alarmingly clear that this fire meant business.

The wind increased greatly, as it always does once a bush fire gets a start; the air was thick with smoke, and full of flying things; in the bush and grass about us there was a constant scurrying; the terror of stampede was in the very atmosphere. A few words of consultation decided us, and we started to burn a patch for standing room and protection.

The hot sun and strong wind had long evaporated all the dew and moisture from the grass, but the sap was still up, and the fire – our fire – seemed cruelly long in catching on. With bunches of dry grass for brands we started burns in twenty places over a length of a hundred yards, and each little flame licked up, spread a little, and then hesitated or died out: it seemed as if ours would never take, while the other came on with roars and leaps, sweeping clouds of sparks and ash over us in the dense rolling mass of smoke.

At last a fierce rush of wind struck down on us, and in a few seconds each little flame became a living demon of destruction; another minute, and the stretch before us was a field of swaying flame. There was a sudden roar and crackle, as of musketry, and the whole mass seemed lifted into the air in one blazing sheet: it simply leaped into life and swept everything before it.

When we opened our scorched eyes the ground in front of us was all black, with only here and there odd lights and torches about – like tapers on a pall; and on ahead, beyond the trellis work of bare scorched trees, the wall of flame swept on.

Then down on the wings of the wind came the other fire; and before it fled every living thing. Heaven only knows what passed us in those few minutes when a broken stream of terrified creatures dashed by, hardly swerving to avoid us. There is no coherent picture left of that scene – just a medley of impressions linked up by flashes of unforgettable vividness. A herd of koodoo came crashing by; I know there was a herd, but only the first and last will come to mind – the space between seems blurred. The clear impressions are of the koodoo bull in front, with nose out-thrust, eyes shut against the bush, and great horns laid back upon the withers, as he swept along opening the way for his herd; and then, as they vanished, the big ears, ewe neck, and tilting hind-quarters of the last cow – between them nothing but a mass of moving grey!

The wildebeeste went by in Indian file, uniform in shape, colour and horns; and strangely uniform in their mechanical action, lowered heads, and fiercely determined rush.

A rietbuck ram stopped close to us, looked back wide-eyed and anxious, and whistled shrilly, and then cantered on with head erect and white tail flapping; but its mate neither answered nor came by. A terrified hare with its ears laid flat scuttled past within a yard of Francis and did not seem to see him. Above us scared birds swept or fluttered down wind; while others again came up swirling and swinging about, darting boldly through the smoke to catch the insects driven before the fire.

But what comes back with the suggestion of infinitely pathetic helplessness is the picture of a beetle. We stood on the edge of our burn, waiting for the ground to cool, and at my feet a pair of tock-tockie beetles, hump backed and bandy legged, came toiling slowly and earnestly along; they reached the edge of our burn, touched the warm ash, and turned patiently aside – to walk round it!

A school of chattering monkeys raced out on to the blackened flat, and screamed shrilly with terror as the hot earth and cinders burnt their feet.

Porcupine, antbear, meerkat! They are vague, so vague that nothing is left but the shadow of their passing; but there is one other thing – seen in a flash as brief as the others, for a second or two only, but never to be forgotten! Out of the yellow grass, high up in the waving tops, came sailing down on us the swaying head and glittering eyes of a black mamba – swiftest, most vicious, most deadly of snakes. Francis and I were not five yards apart and it passed between us, giving a quick chilly beady look at each – pitiless, and hateful – and one hiss as the slithering tongue shot out: that was all, and it sailed past with strange effortless movement. How much of the body was on the ground propelling it, I cannot even guess; but we had to look upwards to see the head as the snake passed between us.

The scorching breath of the fire drove us before it on to the baked ground, inches deep in ashes and glowing cinders, where we kept marking time to ease our blistering feet; our hats were pulled down to screen our necks as we stood with our backs to the coming flames; our flannel shirts were so hot that we kept shifting our shoulders for relief. Jock, who had no screen and whose feet had no protection, was in my arms; and we strove to shield ourselves from the furnace-blast with the branches we had used to beat out the fire round the big tree which was our main shelter.

The heat was awful! Live brands were flying past all the time, and some struck us: myriads of spark fell round and on us, burning numberless small holes in our clothing, and dotting blisters on our backs: great sheets of flame leaped out from the driving glare, and, detached by many yards from their source, were visible for quite a space in front of us. Then, just at its maddest and fiercest, there came a gasp and sob, and the fire devil died behind us as it reached the black bare ground. Our burn divided it as an island splits the flood, and it swept along our flanks in two great walls of living leaping roaring flame.

Two hundred yards away there was a bare yellow place in a world of inky black, and to that haven we ran. It was strange to look about and see the naked country all round us, where but a few minutes earlier the tall grass had shut us in; but the big bare ant-heap was untouched, and there we flung ourselves down, utterly done.

Faint from heat and exhaustion – scorched and blistered, face and arms, back and feet; weary and footsore, and with boots burnt through – we reached camp long after dark, glad to be alive.

We had forgotten the wounded buffalo; he seemed part of another life!

Percy Fitzpatrick (1862–1931), *Jock of the Bushveld*

TOO CLOSE TO THE SUN

Ransom is a student of languages who is kidnapped by Weston and Devine, and for purposes of theirs is secretly taken by space-ship to Malacandra, a planet inhabited by three races of beings. For the journey back to earth they have ninety days. The benevolent ruling spirit of Malacandra had rendered the two conspirators harmless, and has promised to destroy the space-ship soon after its return to Earth.

It was well for him that he had reached this frame of mind before the real hardships of their journey began. Ever since their departure from Malacandra, the thermometer had steadily risen; now it was higher than it had stood at any time on their outward journey. And still it rose. The light also increased. Under his glasses he kept his eyes habitually tight shut, opening them only for the shortest time for necessary movements. He knew that if he reached Earth it would be with permanently damaged sight. But all this was nothing to the torment of heat. All three of them were awake for twenty-four hours out of the twenty-four, enduring with dilated eye-balls, blackened lips and froth-flecked cheeks the agony of thirst. It would be madness to increase their scanty rations of water: madness even to consume air in discussing the question.

He saw well enough what was happening. In his last bid for life Weston was venturing inside the Earth's orbit, leading them nearer the Sun than man, perhaps than life, had ever been. Presumably this was unavoidable; one could not follow a retreating Earth round the rim of its own wheeling course. They must be trying to meet it – to cut across . . . it was madness! But the question did not much occupy his mind; it was not possible for long to think of anything but thirst. One thought of water; then one thought of thirst; then one thought of thinking of thirst; then of water again. And still the thermometer rose. The walls of the ship were too hot to touch. It was obvious that a crisis was approaching. In the next few hours it must kill them or get less.

It got less. There came a time when they lay exhausted and shivering in what seemed the cold, though it was still hotter than any terrestrial climate. Weston had so far succeeded; he had risked the highest temperature at which human life could theoretically survive, and they had lived through it. But they were not the same men. Hitherto Weston had slept very little even in his watches off; always, after an hour or so of uneasy rest, he had returned to his charts and to his endless, almost despairing, calculations. You could see him fighting the despair – pinning his terrified brain down, and again down, to the figures. Now he never looked at them. He even seemed careless in the control room. Devine moved and looked like a somnambulist. Ransom lived increasingly on the dark side and for long hours he thought of nothing. Although the first great danger was past, none of them, at this time, had any serious hope of a successful issue to their journey. They had now been fifty days, without speech, in their steel shell, and the air was already very bad.

Weston was so unlike his old self that he even allowed Ransom to take his share in the navigation. Mainly by signs, but with the help of a few whispered words, he taught him all that was necessary at this stage of the journey. Apparently they were racing home – but with little chance of reaching it in time – before some sort of cosmic 'trade-wind'. A few rules of thumb enabled Ransom to keep the star which Weston pointed out to him in its position at the centre of the skylight, but always with his left hand on the bell to Weston's cabin.

This star was not the Earth. The days – the purely theoretical 'days' which bore such a desperately practical meaning for the travellers – mounted to fifty-eight before Weston changed course, and a different luminary was in the centre. Sixty days, and it was visibly a planet. Sixty-six, and it was like a planet seen through field-glasses. Seventy, and it was like nothing that Ransom had ever seen – a little dazzling disk too large for a planet and far too small for the Moon. Now that he was navigating, his celestial mood was shattered. Wild, animal thirst for life, mixed with homesick longing for the free airs and the sights and smells of earth – for grass and meat and beer and tea and the human voice – awoke in him. At first his chief difficulty on watch had been to resist drowsiness; now, though the air was worse, feverish excitement kept him vigilant. Often when he came off duty he found right arm stiff and sore; for hours he had been pressing it unconsciously against the control board as if his puny thrust could spur the space-ship to yet greater speed.

Now they had twenty days to go. Nineteen – eighteen – and on the white terrestrial disk, now a little larger than a sixpence, he thought he could make out Australia and the south-east corner of Asia. Hour after hour, though the markings moved slowly across the disk with the Earth's diurnal revolution, the disk itself to grow larger. 'Get on! Get on!' Ransom muttered to the ship. Now ten days were left and it was like the Moon and so bright that they could not look steadily at it. The air in their little sphere was ominously bad, but Ransom and Devine risked a whisper as they changed watches.

'We'll do it,' they said. 'We'll do it yet.'

On the eighty-seventh day, when Ransom relieved Devine, he thought there was something wrong with the Earth. Before his watch was done, he was sure. It was no longer a true circle, but bulging a little on one side; it was almost pear-shaped. When Weston came on duty he gave one glance at the skylight, rang furiously on the bell for Devine, thrust Ransom aside, and took the navigating seat. His face was the colour of putty. He seemed to be about to do something to the controls, but as Devine entered the room he looked up and shrugged his shoulders with a gesture of despair. Then he buried his face in his hands and laid his head down on the control-board.

Ransom and Devine exchanged glances. They bundled Weston out of the seat – he was crying like a child – and Devine took his place. And now at last Ransom understood the mystery of the bulging Earth. What had appeared as a bulge on one side of her disk was becoming increasingly distinct as a second disk, a disk almost as large in appearance as her own. It was covering more than half of the Earth. It was the Moon – between them and the Earth, and two hundred and forty thousand miles nearer. Ransom did not know what fate this might mean for the space-ship. Devine obviously did, and never had he appeared so admirable. His face was as pale as Weston's, but his eyes were clear and preternaturally bright; he sat crouched over the controls like an animal about to spring and he was whistling very softly between his teeth.

Hours later Ransom understood what was happening. The

Moon's disk was now larger than the Earth's, and very gradually it became apparent to him that both disks were diminishing in size. The space-ship was no longer approaching either the Earth or the Moon; it was farther away from them than it had been half an hour ago, and that was the meaning of Devine's feverish activity with the controls. It was not merely that the Moon was crossing their path and cutting them off from the Earth; apparently for some reason – probably gravitational – it was dangerous to get too close to the Moon, and Devine was standing off into space. In sight of harbour they were being forced to turn back to the open sea. He glanced up at the chronometer. It was the morning of the eighty-eighth day. Two days to make the Earth, and they were moving away from her.

'I suppose this finishes us?' he whispered.

'Expect so,' whispered Devine, without looking round.

Weston presently recovered sufficiently to come back and stand beside Devine. There was nothing for Ransom to do. He was sure, now, that they were soon to die. With this realization, the agony of his suspense suddenly disappeared. Death, whether it came now or some thirty years later on earth, rose up and claimed his attention. There are preparations a man likes to make. He left the control room and returned into one of the sunward chambers, into the indifference of the moveless light, the warmth, the silence, and the sharp-cut shadows. Nothing was farther from his mind than sleep. It must have been the exhausted atmosphere which made him drowsy. He slept.

He awoke in almost complete darkness in the midst of a loud continuous noise, which he could not at first identify. It reminded him of something – something he seemed to have heard in a previous existence. It was a prolonged drumming noise close above his head. Suddenly his heart gave a great leap.

'Oh God,' he sobbed. 'Oh God! It's rain.'

He was on Earth. The air was heavy and stale about him, but the choking sensations he had been suffering were gone. He realized that he was still in the spaceship. The others, in fear of its threatened 'unbodying', had characteristically abandoned it the moment it touched Earth and left him to his fate. It was difficult in the dark, and under the crushing weight of terrestrial gravity, to find his way out. But he managed it. He found the manhole and slithered, drinking great draughts of air, down the outside of the sphere; slipped in mud, blessed the smell of it, and at last raised the unaccustomed weight of his body to its feet. He stood in pitch-black night under torrential rain. With every pore of his body he drank it in; with every desire of his heart he embraced the smell of the field about him – a patch of his native planet where grass grew, where cows moved, where presently he would come to hedges and a gate.

He had walked about half an hour when a vivid light behind him and a strong, momentary wind informed him that the space-ship was no more. He felt very little interest. He had seen dim lights of men, ahead. He contrived to get into a lane, then into a road, then into a village street. A lighted door was open. There were voices from within and they were speaking English. There was a familiar smell. He pushed his way in, regardless of the surprise he was creating, and walked to the bar.

'A pint of bitter, please,' said Ransom.

C. S. Lewis (1898–1965), *Out of the Silent Planet*

3

GIRLS AND WOMEN

AFRICAN HOSPITALITY

Mungo Park was a Scotsman, who was at first a ship's surgeon. Then in 1795 he was employed by the African Association to explore the River Niger. Ten years later, on another expedition, he was killed by Africans at the age of 35.

I waited more than two hours, without having an opportunity of crossing the river; during which time the people who had crossed, carried information to Mansong the King, that a white man was waiting for a passage, and was coming to see him. He immediately sent over one of his chief men, who informed me that the king could not possibly see me, until he knew what had brought me into his country; and that I must not presume to cross the river without the king's permission. He therefore advised me to lodge at a distant village, to which he pointed, for the night; and said that in the morning he would give me further instructions how to conduct myself. This was very discouraging. However, as there was no remedy, I set off for the village; where I found, to my great mortification, that no person would admit me into his house. I was regarded with astonishment and fear, and was obliged to sit all day without victuals, in the shade of a tree; and the night threatened to be very uncomfortable, for the wind rose, and there was great appearance of a heavy rain; and the wild beasts are so very numerous in the neighbourhood, that I should have been under the necessity of climbing up the tree, and resting amongst the branches. About sunset, however, as I was preparing to pass the night in this manner, and had turned my horse loose, that he might graze at liberty, a woman, returning from the labours of the field, stopped to observe me, and perceiving that I was weary and dejected, inquired into my situation, which I briefly explained to her; whereupon, with looks of great compassion,

69

she took up my saddle and bridle, and told me to follow her.
Having conducted me into her hut, she lighted up a lamp,
spread a mat on the floor, and told me I might remain there for
the night. Finding that I was very hungry, she said she would
procure me something to eat. She accordingly went out, and
returned in a short time with a very fine fish; which, having
caused to be half broiled upon some embers, she gave me for
supper. The rites of hospitality being thus performed towards a
stranger in distress, my worthy benefactress (pointing to the mat,
and telling me I might sleep there without apprehension) called
to the female part of her family, who had stood gazing on me all
the while in fixed astonishment, to resume their task of spinning
cotton; in which they continued to employ themselves great part
of the night. They lighted their labour by songs, one of which
was composed extempore; for I was myself the subject of it. It
was sung by one of the young women, the rest joining in a sort
of chorus. The air was sweet and plaintive, and the words, liter-
ally translated, were these. – 'The winds roared, and the rains
fell. The poor white man, faint and weary, came and sat under
our tree. He has no mother to bring him milk; no wife to grind
his corn. *Chorus*. Let us pity the white man; no mother has he,
&c. &c.' Trifling as this recital may appear to the reader, to a
person in my situation, the circumstance was affecting in the
highest degree. I was oppressed by such unexpected kindness;
and sleep fled from my eyes. In the morning I presented my
compassionate landlady with two of the four brass buttons which
remained on my waistcoat; the only recompense I could make
her.

Mungo Park (1771-1806), *Travels in the Interior of Africa*

TWO ORPHAN FLOWER GIRLS

Henry Mayhew took immense pains to find out for himself the truth about the poor and unfortunate in London. He wrote several volumes on his researches, his aim all the time being to improve the lot of those who so often managed to remain cheerful and human in terrible conditions.

Of these girls the elder was fifteen and the younger eleven. Both were clad in old, but not torn, dark print frocks, hanging so closely, and yet so loosely, about them as to show the deficiency of under-clothing; they wore old broken black chip bonnets. The older sister (or rather half-sister) had a pair of old worn-out shoes on her feet, the younger was barefoot, but trotted along, in a gait at once quick and feeble – as if the soles of her little feet were impervious, like horn to the roughness of the road. The older girl has a modest expression of countenance, with no pretensions to prettiness except in having tolerably good eyes. Her complexion was somewhat muddy, and her features somewhat pinched. The younger child had a round, chubby, and even rosy face, and quite a healthful look . . .

They lived in one of the streets near Drury-lane. They were inmates of a house, not let out as a lodging-house, in separate beds, but in rooms, and inhabited by street-sellers and street-labourers. The room they occupied was large, and one dim candle lighted it so insufficiently that it seemed to exaggerate the dimensions. The walls were bare and discoloured with damp. The furniture consisted of a crazy table and a few chairs, and in the centre of the room was an old four-post bedstead of the larger size. This bed was occupied nightly by the two sisters and their brother, a lad just turned thirteen. In a sort of recess in a corner of the room was the decency of an old curtain – or something equivalent, for I could hardly see in the dimness – and behind this, I presume, was the bed of the married couple. The three children paid 2s. a week for the room, the tenant, an Irishman

71

out of work, paying 2s. 9d., but the furniture was his, and his
wife aided the children in their trifle of washing, mended their
clothes, where such a thing was possible, and such like. The
husband was absent at the time of visit, but the wife seemed of a
better stamp, judging by her appearance, and by her refraining
from any direct, or even indirect, way of begging, as well as from
the 'Glory be to Gods!' 'the heavens be your honour's bed!' or
'it's the truth I'm telling of you, sir,' that I so frequently met with
on similar visits.

The elder girl said, in an English accent, not at all garrulously,
but merely in answer to my questions: 'I sell flowers, sir; we live
almost on flowers when they are to be got. I sell, and so does my
sister, all kinds, but it's very little use offering any that's not
sweet. I think it's the sweetness as sells them. I sell primroses,
when they're in, and violets, and wall-flowers, and stocks, and
roses of different sorts, and pinks, and carnations, and mixed
flowers, and lilies of the valley, and green lavender, and migno-
nette (but that I do very seldom), and violets again at this time
of the year, for we get them both in spring and winter. The best
sale of all is, I think, moss-roses, young moss-roses. We do best
of all on them. Primroses are good, for people say: "Well, here's
spring again to a certainty." Gentlemen are our best customers.
I've heard that they buy flowers to give to the ladies. Ladies have
sometimes said: "A penny, my poor girl, here's three-halfpence for
the bunch." Or they've given me the price of two bunches for one;
so have gentlemen. I never had a rude word said to me by a
gentleman in my life – never. I never go among boys, I know
nobody but my brother. My father was a tradesman in Mitchels-
town, in the County Cork. I don't know what sort of a tradesman
he was. I never saw him. He was a tradesman I've been told. I
was born in London. Mother was a chairwoman, and lived very
well. None of us ever saw a father. We don't know anything
about our fathers. We were all "mother's children." Mother died
seven years ago last Guy Faux day. I've got myself, and my
brother and sister a bit of bread ever since, and never had any
help but from the neighbours. I never troubled the parish. Oh,
yes, sir, the neighbours is all poor people, very poor, some of
them. We've lived with her' (indicating her landlady by a gesture)
'these two years, and off and on before that. I can't say how long.'

'Well, I don't know exactly,' said the landlady, 'but I've had them with me almost all the time, for four years, as near as I can recollect; perhaps more. I've moved three times, and they always followed me.' In answer to my inquiries the landlady assured me that these two poor girls, were never out of doors all the time she had known them after six at night.

'We've always good health. We can all read. I put myself, and I put my brother and sister to a Roman Catholic school – and to Ragged Schools – but *I* could read before mother died. My brother can write, and I pray to God that he'll do well with it.

I buy my flowers at Covent Garden; sometimes, but very seldom, at Farringdon. I pay 1s. for a dozen bunches, whatever flowers are in. Out of every two bunches I can make three, at 1d. a piece. Sometimes one or two over in the dozen, but not so often as I would like. We make up the bunches ourselves. We get the rush to tie them with for nothing. We put their own leaves round these violets. The paper for a dozen costs a penny; sometimes only a halfpenny. The two of us doesn't make less than 6d. a day, unless it's very ill luck. But religion teaches us that God will support us, and if we make less we say nothing. We do better on oranges in March or April, I think it is, than on flowers. Oranges keep better than flowers you see, sir. We make 1s. a day, and 9d. a day, on oranges, the two of us. I wish they was in all the year. I generally go St. John's-wood way, and Hampstead and High-gate way with my flowers. I can get them nearly all the year, but oranges is better liked than flowers, I think.

I always keep 1s. stock-money, if I can. If it's bad weather, so bad that we can't sell flowers at all, and so if we've had to spend our stock-money for a bit of bread, she [the landlady] lends us 1s., if she has one, or she borrows one of a neighbour, if she hasn't, or if the neighbours hasn't it, she borrows it at a dolly-shop [illegal pawn-shop]. There's 2d. a week to pay for 1s. at a dolly, and perhaps an old rug left for it; if it's very hard weather, the rug must be taken at night time, or we are starved with the cold. It sometimes has to be put into the dolly again next morn-ing, and then there's 2d. to pay for it for the day. We've had a frock in for 6d., and that's a penny a week, and the same for a day. We never pawned anything; we have nothing they would take in at the pawnshop.

We live on bread and tea, and sometimes a fresh herring of a night. Sometimes we don't eat a bit all day when we're out;

sometimes we take a bit of bread with us, or buy a bit. My sister can't eat taturs; they sicken her. I don't know what emigrating means. [I informed her and she continued]: No, sir, I wouldn't like to emigrate and leave brother and sister. If they went with me I don't think I should like it, not among strangers. I think our living costs us 2s. a week for the two of us; the rest goes in rent. That's all we make.'

The brother earned from 1s. 6d. to 2s. a week, with an occasional meal, as a costermonger's boy. Neither of them ever missed mass on a Sunday.

Henry Mayhew (1812–1887),
London Labour and the Labouring Poor

A TRAIN OF THE 'SEVENTIES

With her three brothers Mary Hughes enjoyed in London a childhood that lacked only a supply of interesting relatives. The yearly visits to her mother's numerous and attractive relatives in Cornwall made up for this. When she grew up she married and worked in the cause of education for women.

To us children an important element in this piece of luck was the journey of three hundred miles that it involved. Our parents must have thought otherwise. Had they not been peculiarly carefree by disposition they would never have embarked on the adventure of taking five children all that way in a train of the 'seventies. Coaching days were doubtless bad, but there were inns on the way.

We used to go to bed earlier the day before, not so much to please Mother as to bring to-morrow a bit sooner. We got up long before it was necessary, impeding all the sandwich-making and hard-boiling of eggs that was going on. But eat a good breakfast we could not, being 'journey-proud', as our old cook used to express our excited state. Meanwhile the luggage was being assembled in the hall, having its last touches of cording and labels. For weeks I had been packing in my bedroom, and once I presented five large cardboard boxes, wobbly with various belongings. My father ran upstairs to inspect them, and solemnly looking at them said: 'Now, Molly, which of these is really the most important?' Charmed by his businesslike manner and by the word 'important', I gladly pointed to one, and consented to leave the others behind.

The next crisis was the fetching of a cab. At seven o'clock in the morning there was no certainty of getting one quickly, and we kept rushing to the window until someone shouted: 'Here it comes.' If you saw that cab to-day your anxiety would be as to whether it could possibly stay the course to the main line station at Paddington. The few 'growlers' still to be seen in the London streets are royal coaches compared with those of the 'seventies.

They were like the omnibuses, with the same dingy blue velvet, only much dirtier, and as they were used for taking people to hospitals, my father used to call them 'fever-boxes'. To us children no Cinderella's fairy-carriage could have been handsomer than the cab actually at the door. If we were all going my father and the elder boys had to follow in a second cab. Luggage was piled on the top, and we were packed in among rugs, umbrellas, and hand-bags. At last the cabby climbed up to his seat and whipped up the horse. It took an hour or more to jog from Canonbury to Paddington, but we did reach the enchanted spot at last.

The train was scheduled to start at 9 a.m. and to arrive at Camborne at 9 p.m. Luncheon-baskets had not been invented, neither was it possible to reserve seats. In order, therefore, to travel altogether in one compartment we had to arrive more than half an hour before the train was to start. There was then the suspense of waiting for it to come in, and my fear that we might not be on the right platform or that the Great Western Railway had forgotten all about it. My father meanwhile was taking the tickets and having the luggage labelled. Never did he hasten his steps or hurry, no matter was the emergency, so that there was the additional fear that he would miss the train. When at last we were all safely in a carriage, he would saunter off to buy a paper! and other people were coming in.

In time everything was settled and we were gliding out, 'with our faces towards Cornwall', as Mother used to say. Very little of the view from the windows escaped us, and I was privileged to 'kneel up' and report the latest news to the company. No sooner had we fairly left London behind, were gathering speed, and had sated ourselves with fields and hedges for a while, than we began to survey our fellow passengers and make friends with them.

Reading, the first stop, was great fun for those on the near side. What more cheering than to see distracted people looking for seats when we were definitely full up? If we had a vacant seat at any stop Charles would suggest that I should be pushed forward, for anyone on seeing me, he maintained, would try farther on. Or he would ejaculate, as anyone was about to come in: 'No one would think that Barnholt was recovering from measles!' We talk of the confusion of a modern station, but it is orderly peace compared to the rushing about and shouting of those days. The wonder is that we ever moved on again. And yet we didn't dare to leave the carriage, because at any moment the guard might decide that he had had enough.

Didcot had one definite pleasure. We knew that little boys would be going up and down the platform singing out: 'Banbury cakes! Banbury cakes!' And Mother would crane out and buy some.

Thus refreshed we were all agog for our next excitement – the Box Tunnel. The railway cuttings grew higher and higher, and at last we rushed with a piercing whistle into the total darkness of 'the longest tunnel in the world'. The oil lamps (later the gas lamps) were let down from above with much labour only at dusk. There was no thought of lighting up for a tunnel. Old ladies may have been afraid of robbery and murder, but it was a great feature of the day's entertainment to us. By a pre-arranged plan the boys and I rose stealthily and felt our way into one another's places. When the train emerged into the light the elders had a shock, or handsomely pretended that they had.

The charm of Bristol was its appearance of being a half-way house. Not that it was so by any means, but it was the elbow-joint of the journey. The muddle and rush were greater even than at Reading, and we were often kept there for some twenty minutes. Yet we dared not leave the carriage for more than a mere leg-stretch just outside the door. I sucked much pleasure from hanging out at the off-side window, to watch the man tapping the wheels and applying the yellow stuff from his box. Thus I understood what my father meant by calling London butter 'train-oil'.

Some of our company usually left the train at Bristol, so that we had the carriage more or less to ourselves, and could move about more freely. This was specially desirable because there was soon to come a magic moment when a glimpse of the sea was possible, just for the short time when Bridgwater Bay was visible on our right. Then we bowled along the warm sleepy countryside of Somerset, with no excitements beyond fields and cows and tiny villages, mile after mile. This was the strategic point that Mother chose for unveiling dinner. A bulging basket had long been eyed as it sat in the rack. Restaurant cars are boons, and luncheon-baskets have their merry surprises, but for food as a species of rapture nothing compares with sandwiches, eggs, pasties, and turnovers, doled out one by one from napkins, when the supply is severely limited. Oranges in summer were unknown then, as well as all the foreign apples and other fruit to be had in London to-day. We had to slake our thirst with acid-drops and a tiny ration of lemonade. If by any chance a fellow passenger remained we always managed to do some little barter of biscuits or sweets, because strange food is even more pleasant than one's own.

We used to hail Exeter as being 'almost there', for it was in Devon, actually the next county to Cornwall, and definitely 'west'. A quiet dignity pervaded its stations, but we were late. A train in those days was never 'on time'. After Exeter we were all keyed up for the greatest treat of the journey. I have travelled in many show places of Europe and America, but have never been along a piece of line to equal the run from Exeter to Teignmouth. With a magnificent gesture, the Great Western swept us to the sea-side, indeed almost into the sea. Mother remembered a day when the waves had washed into the carriage. The bare possibility of such a thing made this part of the run something of an adventure, and we almost hoped it would happen again.

The sun was always shining at Dawlish, and there was the sea all spread out in dazzling blue. And as if the train knew how to enhance the effect, it would roll in and out of short tunnels in the 'rouge', or red sandstone of Devon. Each time it emerged the sea looked bluer and the rocks more fantastic in shape. However beautiful the inland scenery might be, it seemed dull after this, and after Teignmouth we usually fell asleep. I remember being laid out at length with my head on Mother's lap, and the rest being a blank till the glad sound of 'Here's Plymouth' woke me.

By now it was late afternoon, and you would suppose that here at last would be some chance of tea and a wash in comfort. Ah no! The London train didn't care about Cornwall, there were no through carriages arranged for long-distance people, and we had to change into a local affair, with hard wooden seats, and patronized by a succession of market people with large bundles. By the time we had found this train, seen the luggage shifted, carried along our small parcels, and settled into our seats, there was no time to do more than buy a bag of buns. They had not thought then of allowing people to carry cups of tea into the carriage with them.

If a sun-bonneted market woman got in with us Mother could never resist talking to her, and answering the invariable Cornish question, 'Wheer be 'ee goin'?' Then would follow the astonished, 'From Lunnon, are 'ee? Aw, my deer!'

And now it was growing dusk, and the familiar tin-mine buildings were silhouetted against the sky, and generally darkness had descended before we ran into Camborne more than an hour late. We had become indescribably dirty and tired and hungry. But our reception atoned for all. Countless uncles and aunts and cousins were crowding the platform, and as we got out everyone was exclaiming 'Here they are!' We children were the heroes and the spoilt darlings of the hour. We were bundled into waiting carriages and driven to a royal spread. On one such occasion I remember my cousin Edgar running all the mile and a half by the side of the carriage in the dark, giving us a whoop of joy when a gate into a lane had to be opened for us to pass.

M. Vivian Hughes (1867–1956), *A London Family Chronicle*

MOTHER AND DAUGHTER

Gwen Raverat was the daughter of a professor at Cambridge and his American wife, who had peculiar theories about child education.

By all accounts I was a charming baby. As I have never been considered particularly charming since then, I think it is only just to myself to set this on record. It fairly makes me blush to read the pages of admiration in the old letters – not only those of my mother, but others as well. How I have gone off since then! My mother writes of some visitor at Down: 'For the first time I have met a typical English husband, according to our American ideas, cross, bad-tempered and very prejudiced. . . . But *even he* was charmed by Gwen!' . . .

My mother was always throwing out new ideas; some of them were rather wild; others were so simple and sensible that they very nearly amounted to genius; but the application of them was sometimes rather autocratic. For instance, she rightly held that children should lead a simple life, without over-indulgence. Of course we never had fires in our bedroom, unless we were really ill; but then neither did the grown-ups, so that was all right and fair. In spite of the huge coal fires in the sitting-rooms and the hall, the whole house was much colder and draughtier than would now be considered tolerable.

But surely our feeding was unnecessarily austere? We had porridge for breakfast, with salt, not sugar; and milk to drink. Porridge always reminds me of having breakfast alone with my father, when I was so small that I put the porridge into the spoon with my fingers, while he told me stories in French. My mother came down later, perhaps with the sensible idea of avoiding me and the porridge and the French. There was toast and butter, but I never had anything stronger for breakfast, till I tasted bacon for the first time in my life when I went to stay with Frances, at the age of nearly ten.

It is true that twice a week we had, at the end of breakfast, one piece of toast, spread with a thin layer of that dangerous luxury, Jam. But, of course, not butter, too. Butter and Jam on the same bit of bread would have been an unheard-of indulgence – a disgraceful orgy. The queer thing is that we none of us like it to this very day. But these two glamorous Jam-days have permanently coloured my conception of Sundays and Wednesdays, which are both lovely dark red days. Though Wednesday, being also Drawing Class Day, is much the redder of the two. Sunday's delicious jam colour has been considerably paled down by Church.

Just occasionally our father used to give us, as a breakfast treat, a taste of a special food, called by us Speissums; but by our cousins, Purr Meat. There was a continual controversy over the correct name. Fortnum and Mason called it Hung Beef. Some of it was freshly grated every morning into a fluffy pile on a plate; and you put a bit of toast, butter side down, on it, and some of it stuck on. It was delicious. But that was later on, when the decay of morals set in. Margaret got it when she was quite young. I didn't.

There was only bread-and-butter and milk for tea, as Jam might have weakened our moral fibre; and sponge-cakes when visitors came. One of my major crimes was propensity for nibbling the edges off the sponge-cakes before the visitors arrived. Our cousins did not consider that our tea-parties were very good; they were rather sorry for us. We were generally given one piece of Maple Sugar after tea; my mother imported it from the States. It was delicious, but not nearly enough; and we might not ever buy sweets, which were considered very unwholesome; except, oddly enough, butterscotch out of the penny-in-the-slot machines at the railway stations. There was a blessed theory that the slot machines were pure, that the Railways guaranteed their Virtue. But we did not travel often, so I was obliged to steal sugar whenever I could. Certainly I was greedy, but one really had to do the best one could for oneself, in those days, when sugar was thought to be unwholesome; and fruit, though a pleasant treat, was rather dangerous.

As we grew older, our moral fibre was weakened by having either Jam or very heavy dough-cake for tea. But not both, never both. However, this relaxation was the beginning of the end; under our continual pressure the food laws wore thinner and thinner, till by the time they got down to Billy – who is nine years younger than I am – there were no regulations left at all, and he could eat whatever was going for breakfast and tea, just like the grown-ups themselves. And I cannot see that his character is any the worse for it; in fact, he is probably less greedy than I am. Ah, innocent child, he little knew how much he owed to my self-sacrificing campaign for liberty, equality and fraternity over the victuals.

My mother's attacks of theories were often short, but some of them were permanent. For instance, we were never allowed to drink tea at all; for, as a good American she considered it most dangerously stimulating, though coffee was perfectly harmless. But we always drank great quantities of milk, till suddenly one day, a mischief-making doctor promulgated the revolting theory that all milk must be BOILED! Because of *Germs*; of which we now heard for the first time, and in which we declined to believe. So, when cold, boiled milk, *with the skin on it*, was put before us, there was a regular riot of disgust, and we refused to touch it; and went on refusing – with Nana's covert sympathy – till the vile enactment was allowed to lapse, and the Theory faded back into that limbo where Theories wander, while they are waiting for their next incarnation. And in two or three months' time we were happily drinking our nice, fresh, tuberculous milk again.

That was a short bout, though a sharp one. The Theory that Beef was Bad and Mutton was Good died harder; though even my mother's 'muttonic habits' passed off in time; and the Theory that Gingerbread Pudding gave you cancer caused us very little trouble, as we did not much like Gingerbread Pudding anyhow. But there was a permanent ban on brown sugar, because it was made by negroes, who were dirty. We used to tease her by saying that she thought the negroes' skins were not fast colour, so that the brown came off them. I don't believe she really thought that; but, anyhow, I have been left with an unsatisfied brown-sugar complex to this very day.

My mother would have been a keen teetotaller, if my father had not happened to like wine in moderation. She used to explain to us that he only took it for the good of his digestion; but we knew very well that that was Nonsense. All the same we were not allowed to have brandy-butter with our plum-puddings; and she used to tell us a really shocking story, of how her own mother, when she had to dose her children with castor oil, used to give it in Whisky, in order to make them take a dislike for drink. I believe that my mother felt rather guilty because she did not do the same by us; but mercifully she did not. Castor oil *and* whisky together would really have been too much, so dreadful as they both were! Modern children have no idea of the horrors they have escaped, in not having been brought up on castor oil. We were always having doses of it. 'So safe', they used to say; and yet now the doctors consider it dangerous. Sugar is good now and castor oil bad! How happy those ideas would have made us in our day. But I expect it is only a matter of time, till the wheel comes round again, and the doctors reverse the verdict.

My own especial horrors were *powders*, which modern children don't have either. It was a most unpleasant shock to be woken up, when the elders went to bed, and to have a teaspoonful of pink powder – just like plate-powder – with a dab of jelly on top, suddenly presented under your sleepy nose. The powderiness of it sometimes made me really sick.

Another health theory was that, as sea-bathing was wholesome, salt in our bath-water would do just as well as a visit to the seaside. So some handfuls of Dr Tidman's Sea Salt – little round pebbles – were put into the tub we had in front of the day-nursery fire, twice a week. As the salt was only put in when we got in ourselves it did not have time to melt; and we disliked it exceedingly, because the pebbles were so painful to stand or sit on. I suppose this was pure magic?

Our mother was always faithful to Our Doctor, who was the only good doctor in the world. His lightest word was enshrined like a fly in amber, and remained a gospel truth for ever and ever; and as for Our Dentist, in London, he was practically a god. . . .

Of course, we children had a few theories of our own. One was that the gum of cherry or plum trees was delicious, and must be eaten as a great treat. This is a mistake, as it is quite incredibly nasty; and so is snow with jam, which we also believed to be nice. Another theory was, that if you swallowed the smallest speck of cork, it would swell and swell inside, till it filled you right up and you died. There was also the now disproved idea that bulls were infuriated by red rags; for this reason I used to bite in my supposedly red lips if ever I met the oldest and mildest cow; and I remember carefully concealing the red halfpenny stamps on any letters I might be taking to the post, for the same reason. And of course we believed, as I think all nurses and children do, that if you cut, or even scratched, the fold of skin which joins your thumb and first finger, you got lockjaw at once, and died in agonies.

Another theory of my mother's was that the punishment should fit the crime. And so once, when I had bitten the nurserymaid, I had my mouth washed out with soap and water; and another time when I had slapped her, I had socks tied down over my hands and had to come down to lunch and be fed in public with a spoon, when I was quite old. A dreadful punishment for a shy child. And when I cut off my own hair, I was made to go about with it as it was, for several days, before I was allowed to have it cut properly. 'It looks as if a dog had bitten it off', my mother said, as I sat on her knee. She had a very queer look on her face, and I suddenly realized that she was trying not to laugh at me, which mortified me very much.

I was only once spanked that I can remember. I had been put to rest after lunch on my mother's bed, under the muslin curtains, which fell down from the hanging canopy. Now resting is a foolish theory, from which many parents suffer. It is far too exhausting for children, it is really only suitable for the old. I used to get absolutely worn out inventing games to play during the ages when I was condemned to 'rest'; so that by the time the rest was over, I really did need a rest. However, this time I enjoyed myself, I found on the dressing-table a stick of red lip-salve. The white wall-paper was nearly framed by the bed-curtains; so I began a fine, bold wall-painting, in enormous swoops and circles. It was like frescoing the walls of Heaven. But I was interrupted, and my father was told to spank me with a slipper. It didn't hurt and I did not mind a bit. But I never forgot the joy of wallpainting.

Gwen Raverat (1885–1957), *Period Piece*

TWO LESSONS

*As a young man Sir Arthur Grimble joined the Colonial
Service, and was sent to the Gilbert Islands to learn the art of
governing native peoples.*

I worked hard at my Gilbertese, and could make a crude show of
talking it in four months. It was time then, the Old Man thought,
for me to start learning about native customs. He told me to take
lessons first of all from the kaubure of Tabiang village who had
so gently reproved him. As a beginning, I prepared a list of
questions about how a guest was received by the very best
Baanaban families, and how he ought to behave in reply. Nothing
could have been more apt, as it turned out. Armed with the
questionnaire, I went to the kaubure's house-place in the village
an hour or so before sunset on the day arranged.

A little golden girl of seven, naked save for a wreath of white
flowers on her glossy head, invited me to mount upon the raised
floor of the mwenga. As she spread a fine guest-mat for me to sit
upon, she told me her name was Tebutinnang – Movement-of-
Clouds. Seated cross-legged on another mat, she explained with
gravity that her grandfather had charged her to entertain me with
conversation, should I arrive before his return from fishing. He
would not be very long now; would I like to drink a coconut while
she went on entertaining? When I said yes, please, she climbed
down from the floor, brought in a nut which she had opened under
the trees outside with a cutlass-knife almost as long as herself, sat
down again, and offered it to me cupped in both hands, at arm's
length, with her head a little bowed. 'You shall be blessed,' she
murmured as I took it. I did say 'Thank you' in reply, but even
that was wrong; I should have returned her blessing word for
word, and, after that, I should have returned the nut also, for her
to take the first sip of courtesy; and at last, when I had received
it back, I should have said, 'Blessings and Peace', before beginning to drink the milk. All I did – woe is me! – was to take it,

swig it off, and hand it back one-handed, empty, with another careless 'Thank you.'

She did not rise and run off with it as I expected, but sat on instead, with both arms clasping the nut to her little chest, examining me over the top of it.

'Alas!' she said at last in a shocked whisper, 'Alas! Is that the manners of a young chief of Matang?'

She told me one by one of the sins I have confessed, and I hung my head in shame, but that was not yet the full tale. My final discourtesy had been the crudest of all. In handing back the empty nut, I had omitted to belch aloud.

'How could I know when you did not belch,' she said, 'how *could* I know that my food was sweet to you? See, this is how you should have done it!'

She held the nut towards me with both hands, her earnest eyes fixed on mine, and gave vent to a belch so resonant that it seemed to shake her elfin form from stem to stern.

'That,' she finished, 'is *our* idea of good manners,' and wept for the pity of it.

Her grief was the more bitter because this was the first time her grandfather had ever charged her to receive a guest of his. I could not have let her down more abysmally. But one redeeming course seemed still open: I begged her to give me another chance when grandfather came in, and luckily the idea appealed to her. On his arrival, she sat him on his mat, smiled at me and clambered down from the floor to fetch a nut for each of us. I made no mistakes that time; the volume of my final effort shocked me, but it pleased grandfather profoundly and Movement-of-Cloud clapped her little hands for happiness of heart.

It was in my orders to submit written reports on these lessons to the Old Man. In that way, he said, he could keep track of my doings in the villages. I wrote rather fully about the coconut incident, under the heading 'Honourable Eructation', and for some reason of his own he wanted to check up on it. So, one day, we went together by appointment to the village headman's house for an official try-out, but without announcement of the basic motive. A visit from the Resident Commissioner was a big event, and a lot of relatives were there, the women – even small Movement-of-Cloud – all horribly dressed in mission-school Mother Hubbards. I found that rather daunting; also, the presence of my chief threatened to inhibit my output of good taste at the crucial moment. But when I heard the pusillanimous little compromise of a noise, like a politely frustrated hiccough, that he emitted on handing back his nut, I felt that the crumbling prestige of the Men of Matang was mine alone to save in that exquisite village by the sea. It turned me into the champion of a cause – yes, and my effort was indeed the effort of a champion. Au of the Rising Sun himself could not have bettered it. It astounded even our hosts. Movement-of-Cloud shrieked for joy; the rest were convulsed with mixed passions of laughter and fulfilment; people from other houses came crowding round to share the joke; soon, the whole village was rocking with my excess of good manners; and through it all, I, the undoubted hero of the piece, sat gabbling in vain to convince my livid chief that it was one of nature's relieving accidents, the trick of an ailing stomach, an act of God, anything, anything that might serve to save me for a moment from the glare of his cold eyes.

People are fond of saying that you only have to set your mind on a thing firmly enough and long enough for it to come your way at last. My own experience in the service has (doubtless healthily for me) not always corroborated this encouraging doctrine, but I have found that Circumstance – or Providence, or whatever else you like to call it – has a way of returning quick and funny answers to a man's more unreasonable disgruntlements. I was taking a sunset walk one day, after about a year on Ocean Island, in a state of noble discontent. World War I, which we called the Great War then, was nine months old, and I was to be allowed neither to join up nor to go and do a real he-man's job in the Gilbert group. I had no title whatever to go to an out-district, as I had not yet passed my final examinations; but the luxury of life on Ocean Island (with its electric light, frozen meat, fresh vegetables – all from the Company – and mails every month or so) struck me as unworthy of the times. So also did the mainly clerical nature of my duties. I felt that the Colonial Service was turning out, for me, a very soft kind of service. With these thoughts in mind, I came to the inland village of Buakonikai, embowered among its palms and breadfruit trees on the crest of the island.

Looking ahead down the main avenue between the lines of

dwellings, I saw a crowd collected in the open space up against the village *maneaba* (speak-house). The gathering was unusual for that time of day, because the sunset hour belonged by custom to the evening meal. They stood in a wide ring, so intent upon something at the centre that nobody noticed me until I touched an elderly man's shoulder. But, when he turned and saw me, he caught my hand in his and drew me forward.

'Look, all of you!' he cried, 'the Young Man of Matang has arrived!'

They evidently felt that my arrival had solved some problem for them, and when they had made a way through for me, I saw what it was.

A naked man of quite outrageous size (or so it seemed to me) was squatting on his heels at the centre of the circle. His shoulders were crouched forward so that his armpits were propped by his knees. His lank hair was in wild disorder, and he had smeared dust on the sweat of his face. A small knife dangled idly from his left hand; in his right was a cutlass, with which he was slashing around at objects in the air apparently visible to himself, though not to us. His teeth were bared in a rictus that struck me as even more sinister than the worst my Old Man had ever directed at me. But he took not the smallest notice of the crowd. It was as if we were not there for him, except that it stuck out of him about as plainly as death that he was alive to every movement we made.

'This man is mad,' explained my companions, quite unnecessarily, and added, 'we hope you will now bring him to reason for us.'

It appeared that bringing him to reason meant leading him to some place where he could be safely guarded until the fit was over.

'He will not resist you,' they assured me comfortably: 'Ourselves he would resist, for he has taken up his knives against us, and it would shame him now not to use them. Therefore, if we go to take him, we must use sticks and knives for our own defence; and this would not be suitable, for we are many, and he is mad, and we should probably kill him, and he is our brother.'

Their conviction that he could not possibly dream of doing violence to me was based upon the one fact that I was a Man of Matang. Not even a madman could forget that, they said. All I had to do was to approach him, take his hands in mine and say,

'Sir, I beg you to come with me.' The point was, I must not forget to use those words 'I beg you'. The high honour of being thus formally entreated by a chief of Matang would probably heal his sick mind at once, as well as oblige him to obey my every wish after that. The bigger the audience, of course, the more excellent the honour would seem to him. They would, therefore, sit in a semi-circle before him, while I went forward to do the doings.

They rushed around collecting fallen coconut leaves to sit upon, while I was left standing to survey my problem. He was still squatting and slashing the air. He must have heard every word of the excited talk, but he gave no sign whatever of appreciating my honourable intentions. The quality of his grin seemed, if anything, even more threatening than before. I could not help feeling that his chivalry towards me was definitely inferior to that of his fellows towards himself. I must confess also to wondering how soon it would be decent for me to get those saving words 'I beg you' said. Was it absolutely *de rigueur* for me to walk right up to him and lay my hands on his before uttering them? Surely this was a most unreasonable stipulation. But my craven thoughts were cut short: 'We are ready,' called a voice, and the babble of talking ceased. The courteous ceremony was now open.

I trod the first fifteen yards or so as delicately as Agag before his murderous Prophet. My eyes saw nothing but the whirling knife. If he didn't stop flourishing it when I got near him, what was I going to do? Walk right into it? My legs began to feel more stick-like even than they were. Oh, *shut up*, shouted my mind, and blacked out. I had no thoughts whatever for the last few paces.

He kept it up, with his teeth bared, until I was within a yard of him. Then he suddenly relaxed and smiled up at me. As I laid my hands on his wrists, I thought I had never seen such a welcome smile in my life before; but I did wish he would drop those knives. He did nothing of the kind; after I had said my piece, he got up, still holding them, and flung his arms round my neck. I heard a murmur of joyful approbation burst from the audience. This was evidently a good show, so far. But for that reassurance, I should have struggled to break out of his grip, for it was throttling me, and the little knife was round by my left ear, and the big one was searching my right ribs, and he was making inarticulate

noises in his throat. The longer it went on, and the unhappier I
felt, the happier the crowd became, and the longer it went on.
When at last he found words, it was to bawl over my shoulder,
'O, Young Man of Matang, I love thee, I love thee!' This was the
only protestation of its kind I had ever received from a male, and
I did not really enjoy it; but the villagers groaned with delight,
'O, joy! O, blessings! He loves, he loves the Young Man of
Matang,' and that encouraged him to further declarations of
affection. My face was by this time purple and my hair, in every
sense, on end. I don't know how much longer I could have born
the ignominy and terror of it; I don't think the audience would
ever have intervened to cut short that riot of improving emotion.
It was a sudden new arrival among them that saved me. The first
thing I knew about it was the voice of a little girl shrilling from
behind my back, 'Shameless, shameless Barane!' At once, my
neck was released from the strange-hold. I flung his limp arms
from my shoulders. Barane stood alone with hanging head before
the little girl. She was about twelve years old, and flaming with
righteous anger. They told me she was his mother's brother's
daughter, and he had been her special charge for several years.
She certainly knew how to order him about.

'Give me those knives at once,' she shouted, and he surrendered
them.

'Now tell this company you are sorry.'

He did.

'Now tell the Young Man of Matang you are sorry.'

He hesitated a little, and then murmured, 'I love, I love the
Young Man of Matang. I wish him to go with me.'

'He shall lead you home,' she replied, without consulting me,
'take hold of his hand.' The order was addressed as much to
myself as to him. I meekly obeyed it. It would be hard to say
which of us looked the more sheepish as she drove us together,
hand-in-hand before her, down the village street. I felt I must
surely be living up to Mr Johnson's doctrine about the humility
of leadership, but the thought gave me little or no sense of
dignity.

When he was safely installed at home, I ventured to ask a group
of villagers why they had not thought of fetching the little girl at
once, instead of giving the job to me, a stranger. They had a
perfect answer to that, from their point of view. Their case was

that they certainly would have fetched her in the ordinary course, but my sudden arrival had placed an obligation on them. As a chief of Matang, I had the right to the first word and the last word in all things; therefore, the only possible course in politeness was to surrender to me the honour of handling the situation for Barane's family. And besides, it was somehow *kamaiu* (enlivening) when a Man of Matang shared their difficulties with them – much more kamaiu than when they worked alone. I gathered from this that they felt I had enjoyed the evening's fun as much as they had. I did not trouble to disabuse them and, for the rest, what objection could I possibly have urged against their generous courtesy of heart towards my race?

Arthur Grimble (1888–1956), *A Pattern of Islands*

THERE WAS SOMEONE CRYING!

Mary was the child of parents who died of cholera in India, both on the same day. Looked after by Indian servants, she became rather a disagreeable child. She was brought from India to live in a large house in a remote part of Yorkshire. Here she found a walled-up garden; the novel tells how she got in and what she discovered there.

The next day the rain poured down in torrents again, and when Mary looked out of her window the moor was almost hidden by grey mist and cloud. There could be no going out today.

'What do you do in your cottage when it rains like this?' she asked Martha.

'Try to keep from under each other's feet mostly,' Martha answered. 'Eh! there does seem a lot of us then. Mother's a good-tempered woman, but she gets fair moithered. The biggest ones goes out in th' cow-shed and plays there. Dickon he doesn't mind th' wet. He goes out just th' same as if th' sun was shinin'. He says he sees things on rainy days as doesn't show when it's fair weather. He once found a little fox cub half drowned in its hole and he brought it home in th' bosom of his shirt to keep it warm. Its mother had been killed near by an' th' hole was swum out an' th' rest o' th' litter was dead. He's got it at home now. He found a half-drowned young crow another time an' he brought it home, too, an' tamed it. It's named Soot, because it's so black an' it hops an' flies about with him everywhere.'

The time had come when Mary had forgotten to resent Martha's familiar talk. She had even begun to find it interesting and to be sorry when she stopped or went away. The stories she had been told by her Ayah when she lived in India had been quite unlike those Martha had to tell about the moorland cottage which held fourteen people who lived in four little rooms and never had quite enough to eat. The children seemed to tumble about and amuse themselves like a litter of rough, good-natured

collie puppies. Mary was most attracted by the mother and
Dickon. When Martha told stories of what 'mother' said or did
they always sounded comfortable.

'If I had a raven or a fox cub I could play with it,' said Mary.
'But I have nothing.'

Martha looked perplexed.

'Can tha' knit?' she asked.

'No,' answered Mary.

'Can tha' sew?'

'No.'

'Can tha' read?'

'Yes.'

'Then why doesn't tha' read somethin' or learn a bit o'
spellin'? Tha'st old enough to be learnin' thy book a good bit
now.'

'I haven't any books,' said Mary. 'Those I had were left in
India.'

'That's a pity,' said Martha. 'If Mrs Medlock'd let thee go int'
th' library, there's thousands o' books there.'

Mary did not ask where the library was, because she was suddenly inspired by a new idea. She made up her mind to go and
find it herself. She was not troubled about Mrs Medlock. Mrs
Medlock seemed always to be in her comfortable housekeeper's
sitting-room downstairs. In this queer place one scarcely ever
saw anyone at all. In fact, there was no one to see but the servants,
and when their master was away they lived a luxurious life below
stairs, where there was a huge kitchen hung about with shining
brass and pewter, and a large servants' hall where there were four
or five abundant meals eaten every day, and where a great deal
of lively romping went on when Mrs Medlock was out of the
way.

Mary's meals were served regularly, and Martha waited on her,
but no one troubled themselves about her in the least. Mrs Medlock came and looked at her every day or two, but no one inquired what she did or told her what to do. She supposed that
perhaps this was the English way of treating children. In India
she had always been attended by her Ayah, who had followed her
about and waited on her, hand and foot. She had often been tired
of her company. Now she was followed by nobody and was learning to dress herself, because Martha looked as though she thought

she was silly and stupid when she wanted to have things handed to her and put on.

'Hasn't tha' got good sense?' she said once, when Mary had stood waiting for her to put on her gloves for her. 'Our Susan Ann is twice as sharp as thee an' she's only four year' old. Sometimes tha' looks fair soft in th' head.'

Mary had worn her contrary scowl for an hour after that, but it made her think several entirely new things.

She stood at the window for about ten minutes this morning after Martha had swept up the hearth for the last time and gone downstairs. She was thinking over the new idea which had come to her when she heard of the library. She did not care very much about the library itself, because she had read very few books; but to hear of it brought back to her mind the hundred rooms with closed doors. She wondered if they were all really locked and what she would find if she could get into any of them. Were there a hundred really? Why shouldn't she go and see how many doors she could count? It would be something to do on this morning when she could not go out. She had never been taught to ask permission to do things, and she knew nothing at all about authority, so she would not have thought it necessary to ask Mrs Medlock if she might walk about the house, even if she had seen her.

She opened the door of the room and went into the corridor, and then she began her wanderings. It was a long corridor and it branched into other corridors and it led her up short flights of steps which mounted to others again. There were doors and doors, and there were pictures on the walls. Sometimes they were pictures of dark, curious landscapes, but oftenest they were portraits of men and women in queer, grand costumes made of satin and velvet. She found herself in one long gallery whose walls were covered with those portraits. She had never thought there could be so many in any house. She walked slowly down this place and stared at the faces, which also seemed to stare at her. She felt as if they were wondering what a little girl from India was doing in their house. Some were pictures of children – little girls in thick satin frocks which reached to their feet and stood out about them, and boys with puffed sleeves and lace collars and long hair, or with big ruffs around their necks. She always stopped to look at the children, and wonder what their names were, and where they had gone, and why they wore such odd clothes. There was a stiff, plain little girl rather like herself. She wore a green brocade dress and held a green parrot on her finger. Her eyes had a sharp, curious look.

'Where do you live now?' said Mary aloud to her. 'I wish you were here.'

Surely no other little girl ever spent such a queer morning. It seemed as if there was no one in all the huge, rambling house but her own small self, wandering about upstairs and down, through narrow passages and wide ones, where it seemed to her that no one but herself had ever walked. Since so many rooms had been built, people must have lived in them, but it all seemed so empty that she could not quite believe it true.

It was not until she climbed to the second floor that she thought of turning the handle of a door. All the doors were shut, as Mrs Medlock had said they were, but at last she put her hand on the handle of one of them and turned it. She was almost frightened for a moment when she felt that it turned without difficulty and that when she pushed upon the door itself it slowly and heavily opened. It was a massive door and opened into a big bedroom. There were embroidered hangings on the wall, and inlaid furniture such as she had seen in India stood about the room. A broad window with leaded panes looked out upon the moor; and over the mantel was another portrait of the stiff, plain little girl who seemed to stare at her more curiously than ever.

'Perhaps she slept here once,' said Mary. 'She stares at me so that she makes me feel queer.'

After that she opened more doors and more. She saw so many rooms that she became quite tired and began to think that there must be a hundred, though she had not counted them. In all of them there were old pictures or old tapestries with strange scenes worked on them. There were curious pieces of furniture and curious ornaments in nearly all of them.

In one room, which looked like a lady's sitting-room, the hangings were all embroidered velvet, and in a cabinet were about a hundred little elephants made of ivory. They were of different sizes, and some had their mahouts or palanquins on their backs. Some were much bigger than the others and some were so tiny that they seemed only babies. Mary had seen carved ivory in India and she knew all about the elephants. She opened the door

of the cabinet and stood on a footstool and played with these for
quite a long time. When she got tired she set the elephants in
order and shut the door of the cabinet.

In all her wanderings through the long corridors and the empty
rooms she had seen nothing alive; but in this room she saw something. Just after she had closed the cabinet door she heard a tiny
rustling sound. It made her jump and look around at the sofa by
the fireplace, from which it seemed to come. In the corner of the
sofa there was a cushion, and in the velvet which covered it there
was a hole, and out of the hole peeped a tiny head with a pair of
frightened eyes in it.

Mary crept softly across the room to look. The bright eyes
belonged to a little grey mouse, and the mouse had eaten a hole
into the cushion and made a comfortable nest there. Six baby
mice were cuddled up asleep near her. If there was no one else
alive in the hundred rooms there were seven mice who did not
look lonely at all.

'If they wouldn't be so frightened I would take them back with
me,' said Mary.

She had wandered about long enough to feel too tired to
wander any further, and she turned back. Two or three times she
lost her way by turning down the wrong corridor and was obliged
to ramble up and down until she found the right one; but at last
she reached her own floor again, though she was some distance
from her own room and did not know exactly where she was.

'I believe I have taken a wrong turning again,' she said, standing still at what seemed the end of a short passage with tapestry
on the wall. 'I don't know which way to go. How still everything is!'

It was while she was standing here and just after she had said
this that the stillness was broken by a sound. It was another cry,
but not quite like the one she had heard last night; it was only a
short one, a fretful, childish whine muffled by passing through
walls.

'It's nearer than it was,' said Mary, her heart beating rather
faster. 'And it *is* crying.'

She put her hand accidentally upon the tapestry near her, and
then sprang back, feeling quite startled. The tapestry was the
covering of a door which fell open and showed her that there was
another part of the corridor behind it, and Mrs Medlock was

coming up it with her bunch of keys in her hand and a very cross look on her face.

'What are you doing here?' she said, and she took Mary by the arm and pulled her away. 'What did I tell you?'

'I turned round the wrong corner,' explained Mary. 'I didn't know which way to go and I heard someone crying.'

She quite hated Mrs Medlock at the moment, but she hated her more the next.

'You didn't hear anything of the sort,' said the housekeeper. 'You come along back to your own nursery or I'll box your ears.'

And she took her by the arm and half pushed half pulled her up one passage and down another, until she pushed her in at the door of her own room.

'Now,' she said, 'you stay where you're told to stay or you'll find yourself locked up. The master had better get you a governess, same as he said he would. You're one that needs someone to look sharp after you. I've got enough to do.'

She went out of the room and slammed the door after her, and Mary went and sat on the hearth-rug, pale with rage. She did not cry, but ground her teeth.

'There *was* someone crying – there *was* – there *was*!' she said to herself.

She had heard it twice now, and some time she would find out. She had found out a great deal this morning. She felt as if she had been on a long journey, and at any rate she had had something to amuse her all the time, and she had played with the ivory elephants and had seen the grey mouse and its babies in their nest in the velvet cushion.

F. H. Burnett (1849–1924), *The Secret Garden*

4

THIEVES AND DECEIVERS

THE GOOD OLD DAYS?

John Evelyn supported Charles I in the Civil War, travelled on the continent and had many interests. He wrote books on tree-planting, the menace of smoke in London, gardening and architecture. He kept a diary for thirty-two years.

10*th May*   Passing by Smithfield, I saw a miserable creature burning, who had murdered her husband.

29*th.*   I went to give order about a coach to be made against my wife's coming, being my first coach, the pattern whereof I brought out of Paris.

4*th June.*   I set out to meet my wife now on her journey from Paris, after she had obtained leave to come out of that city, which had now been besieged some time by the Prince of Condè's army in the time of the rebellion, and after she had been now near twelve years from her own country, that is, since five years of age, at which time she went over. I went to Rye to meet her, where was an embargo on occasion of the late conflict with the Holland fleet, the two nations being now in war, and which made sailing very unsafe.

11*th June.*   About four in the afternoon, being at bowls on the green, we discovered a vessel which proved to be that in which my wife was, and which got into the harbour about eight that evening, to my no small joy. They had been three days at sea, and escaped the Dutch fleet, through which they passed, taken for fishers, which was great good fortune, there being seventeen bales of furniture and other rich plunder, which I bless God came all safe to land, together with my wife, and my Lady Browne, her mother, who accompanied her. My wife being discomposed by having been so long at sea, we set not forth towards home till the 14th, when hearing the small-pox was very rife in and about

London, and Lady Browne having a desire to drink Tunbridge waters, I carried them thither, and stayed in a very sweet place, private and refreshing, and took the waters myself till the 23rd, when I went to prepare for their reception, leaving them for the present in their little cottage by the Wells.

The weather being hot, and having sent my man on before, I rode negligently under favour of the shade, till, within three miles of Bromley, at a place called the Procession Oak, two cut-throats started out, and striking with long staves at the horse, and taking hold of the reins, threw me down, took my sword, and hauled me into a deep thicket, some quarter of a mile from the highway, where they might securely rob me, as they soon did. What they got of money, was not considerable, but they took two rings, the one an emerald with diamonds, the other an onyx, and a pair of buckles set with rubies and diamonds, which were of value, and after all bound my hands behind me, and my feet, having before pulled off my boots; they then set me up against an oak, with most bloody threats to cut my throat if I offered to cry out, or make any noise; for they should be within hearing, I not being the person they looked for. I told them that if they had not basely surprised me they should not have had so easy a prize, and that it would teach me never to ride near a hedge, since, had I been in the mid-way, they durst not have adventured on me; at which they cocked their pistols, and told me they had long guns, too, and were fourteen companions. I begged for my onyx, and told them it being engraved with my arms would betray them; but nothing prevailed. My horse's bridle they slipped, and searched the saddle, which they pulled off, but let the horse graze, and then turning again bridled him and tied him to a tree, yet so as he might graze, and thus left me bound. My horse was perhaps not taken, because he was marked and cropped on both ears, and well known on that road. Left in this manner, grievously was I tormented with flies, ants, and the sun, nor was my anxiety little how I should get loose in that solitary place, where I could neither hear nor see any creature but my poor horse and a few sheep straggling in the copse.

After near two hours attempting, I got my hands to turn palm to palm, having been tied back to back, and then it was long before I could slip the cord over my wrists to my thumb, which at last I did, and then soon unbound my feet, and saddling my horse and roaming a while about, I at last perceived dust to rise, and soon after heard the rattling of a cart, towards which I made, and, by the help of two countrymen, I got back into the highway. I rode to Colonel Blount's, a great justiciary of the times, who sent out hue and cry immediately. The next morning, sore as my wrists and arms were, I went to London, and got 500 tickets printed and dispersed by an officer of Goldsmiths' Hall, and within two days had tidings of all I had lost, except my sword, which had a silver hilt, and some trifles. The rogues had pawned one of my rings for a trifle to a goldsmith's servant, before the tickets came to the shop, by which means they escaped; the other ring was bought by a victualler, who brought it to a goldsmith, but he having seen the ticket seized the man. I afterwards discharged him on his protestation of innocence. Thus did God deliver me from these villains, and not only so, but restored what they took, as twice before he had graciously done, both at sea and land; I mean when I had been robbed by pirates, and was in danger of a considerable loss at Amsterdam; for which, and many, many signal preservations, I am extremely obliged to give thanks to God my Saviour.

John Evelyn (1620–1706), *Diary*

ILL-GOTTEN GAINS

Best known as the author of Robinson Crusoe, *Daniel Defoe wrote many other books. Here Jack, brought up as a beggar and pickpocket, relates an early adventure.*

Nothing could be more perplexing than this money was to me all that night. I carried it in my hand a good while, for it was in gold, all but 14s.; and that is to say, it was in four guineas, and that 14s. was more difficult to carry than the four guineas; at last I sat down, and pulled off one of my shoes, and put the four guineas into that; but after I had gone a while, my shoe hurt me so I could not go, so I was fain to sit down again, and take it out of my shoe, and carry it in my hand; then I found a dirty linen rag in the street, and I took that up, and wrapped it all together, and carried it in that a good way. I have often since heard people say, when they have been talking of money that they could not get in, 'I wish I had it in a foul clout:' in truth, I had mine in a foul clout; for it was foul, according to the letter of that saying, but it served me till I came to a convenient place, and then I sat down and washed the cloth in the kennel, and so then put my money in again. [*Kennel*, gutter]

Well, I carried it home with me to my lodging in the glass-house, and when I went to go to sleep, I knew not what to do with it; if I had let any of the black crew I was with know of it, I should have been smothered in the ashes for it, or robbed of it, or some trick or other put upon me for it; so I knew not what to do, but lay with it in my hand, and my hand in my bosom, but then sleep went from my eyes . . . Every now and then dropping asleep, I should dream that my money was lost, and start like one frighted; then, finding it fast in my hand, try to go to sleep again, but could not for a long while, then drop and start again. At last a fancy came into my head that if I fell asleep, I should dream of the money and talk of it in my sleep, and tell that I had money, which if I should do, and one of the rogues should hear me, they would pick it out of my bosom, and of my hand too, without waking me; and after that thought I could not sleep a wink more . . . As soon as it was day, I got out of the hole we lay in, and rambled abroad into the fields towards Stepney, and there I mused and considered what I should do with this money, and many a time I wished that I had not had it; for, after all my ruminating upon it, and what course I should take with it, or where I should put it, I could not hit upon any one thing, or any possible method to secure it . . . At last it came into my head, that I would look out for some hole in a tree, and see to hide it there till I should have occasion for it. Big with this discovery, as I then thought it, I began to look about me for a tree; but there were no trees in the fields about Stepney or Mile-End, that looked fit for my purpose; and if there were any, that I began to look narrowly at, the fields were so full of people, that they would see if I went to hide anything there, and I thought the people eyed me as it was, and that two men in particular followed me to see what I intended to do.

This drove me farther off, and I crossed the road at Mile-End, and in the middle of the town went down a lane that goes away to the 'Blind Beggars', at Bethnal-Green; when I came a little way in the lane, I found a footpath over the fields, and in those fields several trees for my turn, as I thought; at last, one tree had a little hole in it, pretty high out of my reach, and I climbed up the tree to get to it, and when I came there, I put my hand in, and found (as I thought) a place very fit, so I placed my treasure there, and was mighty well satisfied with it; but, behold, putting my hand in again to lay it more commodiously, as I thought, of a sudden it slipped away from me, and I found the tree was hollow, and my little parcel was fallen in quite out of my reach, and how far it might go in I knew not; so that, in a word, my money was quite gone, irrecoverably lost; there could be no room so much as to hope ever to see it again, for it was a vast great tree.

As young as I was, I was now sensible what a fool I was before, that I could not think of ways to keep my money, but I must come thus far to throw it into a hole where I could not reach it. Well, I thrust my hand quite up to my elbow, but no bottom was to be found, or any end of the hole or cavity; I got a stick off of the tree, and thrust it in a great way, but all was one; then I cried, nay, I roared out, I was in such a passion; then I got down the tree again, then up again, and thrust in my hand again till I scratched my arm and made it bleed, and cried all the while most violently . . . The last time I had gotten up the tree I happened to come down not on the same side that I went up and came down before, but on the other side of the tree, and on the other side of the bank also; and, behold, the tree had a great open place, in the side of it close to the ground, as old hollow trees often have; and looking into the open place, to my inexpressible joy, there lay my money and my linen rag, all wrapped up just as I had put it into the hole; for the tree being hollow all the way up, there had been some moss or light stuff, which I had not judgement enough to know was not firm, and had given way when it came to drop out of my hand, and so it had slipped quite down at once.

I was but a child, and I rejoiced like a child, for I holloaed quite out aloud when I saw it; then I run to it, and snatched it up, hugged and kissed the dirty rag a hundred times; then danced and jumped about, run from one end of the field to the other, and, in short, I knew not what, much less do I know now what I did, though I shall never forget the thing, either what a sinking grief it was to my heart, when I thought I had lost it, or what a flood of joy overwhelmed me when I had got it again.

II

Well, I came away with my money, and, having taken sixpence out of it, before I made it up again, I went to a chandler's shop in Mile-End, and bought a half-penny roll and a half-pennyworth of cheese, and sat down at the door after I bought it, and ate it very heartily, and begged some beer to drink with it, which the good woman gave me very freely.

Away I went then for the town, to see if I could find any of my companions, and resolved I would try no more hollow trees for my treasure. As I came along Whitechapel, I came by a broker's shop, over against the church, where they sold old clothes, for I had nothing on but the worst of rags; so I stopped at the shop, and stood looking at the clothes which hung at door.

'Well, young gentleman,' says a man that stood at the door, 'you look wishly; do you see anything you like, and will your pocket compass a good coat now, for you look as if you belonged to the ragged regiment?' I was affronted at the fellow. 'What's that to you,' said I, 'how ragged I am? if I had seen anything I liked, I have money to pay for it; but I can go where I shan't be huffed at for looking.'

While I said thus, pretty boldly to the fellow, comes a woman out, 'What ails you,' says she to the man, 'to bully away our customers so? a poor boy's money is as good as my lord mayor's; if poor people did not buy old clothes, what would become of our business?' and then, turning to me, 'Come hither, child,' says she, 'if thou hast a mind to anything I have, you shan't be hectored by him; the boy is a pretty boy, I assure you,' says she, to another woman that was by this time come to her. 'Aye,' says t'other, 'so he is, a very well-looking child, if he was clean and well dressed, and may be as good a gentleman's son for anything we know, as any of those that are well dressed. Come, my dear,' says she, 'tell me what is it you would have?' She pleased me mightily to hear her talk of my being a gentleman's son, and it brought former things to mind; but when she talked of my being not clean, and in rags, then I cried.

She pressed me to tell her if I saw anything that I wanted; I told her no, all the clothes I saw there were too big for me. 'Come, child,' says she, 'I have two things here that will fit you, and I am sure you want them both; that is, first, a little hat, and there,' says she (tossing it to me), 'I'll give you that for nothing; and here is a good warm pair of breeches; I dare say,' says she, 'they will fit you; and they are very tight and good; and,' says she, 'if you should ever come to have so much money that you don't know what to do with it, here are excellent good pockets,' says she, 'and a little fob to put your gold in, or your watch in, when you get it.'

It struck me with a strange kind of joy that I should have a place to put my money in, and need not go to hide it again in a hollow tree; that I was ready to snatch the breeches out of her hands, and wondered that I should be such a fool never to think of buying me a pair of breeches before, that I might have a pocket to put my money in, and not carry it about two days together in my hand, and in my shoe, and I knew not how; so, in a word, I gave her two shillings for the breeches, and went over into the churchyard, and put them on, put my money into my new pockets, and was as pleased as a prince is with his coach and six horses.

Daniel Defoe (1660–1731), *The Life of Colonel Jack*

A ROYAL THIEF

In Shakespeare's King Henry IV (Pt. I) *the King's son, Prince Henry, is shown at first as a good-for-nothing, with the fat braggart Falstaff as his best friend. They plan to rob some travellers, but Falstaff is exposed by the Prince.*

SCENE I

London. An apartment of the Prince's

Prince: Good morrow, Ned.

Poins: Good morrow, sweet Hal. . . . But my lads, my lads, to-morrow morning, by four o'clock, early at Gadshill! there are pilgrims going to Canterbury with rich offerings, and traders riding to London with fat purses: I have vizards for you all; you have horses for yourselves: Gadshill lies to-night in Rochester: I have bespoke supper to-morrow night in East-cheap: we may do it as secure as sleep. If you will go, I will stuff your purses full of crowns; if you will not, tarry at home and be hanged.

Fal: Hear ye, Yedward; if I tarry at home and go not, I'll hang you for going.

Poins: You will, chops?

Fal: Hal, wilt thou make one?

Prince: Who, I rob? I a thief? not I, by my faith.

Fal: There's neither honesty, manhood, nor good fellowship in thee, nor thou camest not of the blood royal, if thou darest not stand for ten shillings.

Prince: Well then, once in my days I'll be a madcap.

Fal: Why, that's well said.

Prince: Well, come what will, I'll tarry at home.

Fal: By the Lord, I'll be a traitor then, when thou art king.

Prince: I care not.

Poins: Sir John, I prithee, leave the prince and me alone: I will lay him down such reasons for this adventure that he shall go.

Fal: Well, God give thee the spirit of persuasion. . . . Farewell: you shall find me in Eastcheap.

Prince: Farewell, thou latter spring! farewell, Allhallown summer!

(*Exit Falstaff*)

Poins: Now, my good sweet honey lord, ride with us to-morrow: I have a jest to execute that I cannot manage alone. Falstaff, Bardolph, Peto and Gadshill shall rob those men that we have already waylaid; yourself and I will not be there; and when they have the booty, if you and I do not rob them, cut this head off from my shoulders.

Prince: How shall we part with them in setting forth?

Poins: Why, we will set forth before or after them, and appoint them a place of meeting, wherein it is at our pleasure to fail, and then will they adventure upon the exploit themselves; which they shall have no sooner achieved, but we'll set upon them.

Prince: Yea, but 'tis like that they will know us by our horses, by our habits, and by every other appointment, to be ourselves.

Poins: Tut! our horses they shall not see; I'll tie them in the wood; our vizards we will change after we leave them: and, sirrah, I have cases of buckram for the nonce, to immask our noted outward garments.

Prince: Yea, but I doubt they will be too hard for us.

Poins: Well, for two of them, I know them to be as true-bred cowards as ever turned back; and for the third, if he fight longer than he sees reason, I'll forswear arms. The virtue of this jest will be, the incomprehensible lies that this same fat rogue will tell us when we meet at supper: how thirty, at least, he fought with; what wards, what blows, what extremities he endured; and in the reproof of this lies the jest.

Prince: Well, I'll go with thee: provide us all things necessary and meet me to-morrow night in Eastcheap; there I'll sup. Farewell.

Poins: Farewell, my lord. . . .

(*Exit*)

Scene II

The highway, near Gadshill

(*Enter Prince Henry and Poins*)

Poins: Come, shelter, shelter: I have removed Falstaff's horse, and he frets like a gummed velvet.

Prince: Stand close.

(*Enter Falstaff*)

Fal: Poins! Poins, and be hanged! Poins!

Prince: Peace, ye fat-kidneyed rascal! what a brawling dost thou keep!

Fal: Where's Poins, Hal?

Prince: He is walked up to the top of the hill; I'll go seek him.

Fal: I am accursed to rob in that thief's company: the rascal hath removed my horse, and tied him I know not where. . . . Well, I doubt not but to die a fair death for all this, if I 'scape hanging for killing that rogue. I have forsworn his company hourly any time this two and twenty years, and yet I am bewitched with the rogue's company. If the rascal have not given me medicines to make me love him, I'll be hanged; it could not be else; I have drunk medicines. Poins! Hal! a plague upon you both! Bardolph! Peto! I'll starve ere I'll rob a foot further. An 'twere not as good a deed as drink, to turn true man and to leave these rogues, I am the veriest varlet that ever chewed with a tooth. Eight yards of uneven ground is threescore and ten miles afoot with me; and the stony-hearted villains know it well enough: a plague upon it when thieves cannot be true one to another! (*They whistle.*) Whew! A plague upon you all! Give me my horse, you rogues; give me my horse, and be hanged!

Prince: Peace, ye fat-guts! lie down; lay thine ear close to the ground and list if thou canst hear the tread of travellers.

Fal: Have you any levers to lift me up again, being down? 'Sblood, I'll not bear mine own flesh so far afoot again for all the coin in thy father's exchequer. What a plague mean ye to colt me thus?

Prince: Thou liest; thou art not colted, thou art uncolted.

Fal: I prithee, good prince Hal, help me to my horse, good king's son.

Prince: Out, ye rogue! shall I be your ostler?

Fal: Go hang thyself in thine own heir-apparent garters! If I be ta'en, I'll peach for this. An I have not ballads made on you all and sung to filthy tunes, let a cup of sack be my poison: when a jest is so forward, and afoot too! I hate it.

(*Enter Gadshill, Bardolph and Peto with him*)

Gads: Stand.

Fal: So I do, against my will.

Poins: O, 'tis our setter: I know his voice. Bardolph, what news?

Bard: Case ye, case ye; on with your vizards: there's money of the king's coming down the hill; 'tis going to the king's exchequer.

Fal: You lie, ye rogue; 'tis going to the king's tavern.

Gads: There's enough to make us all.

Fal: To be hanged.

Prince: Sirs, you four shall front them in the narrow lane; Ned Poins and I will walk lower: if they 'scape from your encounter, then they light on us.

Peto: How many be there of them?

Gads: Some eight or ten.

Fal: 'Zounds, will they not rob us?

Prince: What, a coward, Sir John Paunch?

Fal: Indeed, I am not John of Gaunt, your grandfather; but yet no coward, Hal.

Prince: Well, we leave that to the proof.

Poins: Sirrah Jack, thy horse stands behind the hedge: when thou needest him, there thou shalt find him. Farewell, and stand fast.

Fal: Now cannot I strike him, if I should be hanged.

Prince: Ned, where are our disguises?

Poins: Here, hard by: stand close.

(*Exeunt Prince and Poins*)

Fal: Now, my masters, happy man be his dole, say I: every man to his business.

(*Enter the travellers*)

Frist Trav: Come, neighbour: the boy shall lead our horses down the hill; we'll walk afoot awhile and ease our legs.

Thieves: Stand!

Fal: Strike; down with them; cut the villains' throats: bacon-fed knaves! they hate us youth; down with them; fleece them.

Travellers: O, we are undone, both we and ours for ever!

Fal: Hang ye, gorbellied knaves, are ye undone? No, ye fat chuffs; I would your store were here! On, bacons, on! What, ye knaves! young men must live. You are grand-jurors, are ye? we'll jure ye, 'faith.

(*Here they rob and bind them. Exeunt*)

(*Re-enter Prince Henry and Poins disguised*)

Prince: The thieves have bound the true men. Now could thou and I rob the thieves and go merrily to London, it would be argument for a week, laughter for a month and a good jest for ever.

Poins: Stand close; I hear them coming.

(*Enter the Thieves again*)

Fal: Come, my masters, let us share, and then to horse before day. An the Prince and Poins be not two arrant cowards, there's no equity stirring: there's no more valour in that Poins than in a wild-duck.

Prince: Your money!

Poins: Villains!

(*As they are sharing, the Prince and Poins set upon them; they all run away; and Falstaff, after a blow or two, runs away too, leaving the booty behind them*)

Prince: Got with much ease. Now merrily to horse:

The thieves are all scatter'd and possess'd with fear

So strongly that they dare not meet each other;

Each takes his fellow for an officer.

Away, good Ned. Falstaff sweats to death,

And lards the lean earth as he walks along:

Were't not for laughing, I should pity him.

Poins: How the rogue roar'd!

(*Exeunt*)

Scene III

The Boar's Head in Eastcheap, London

(*Enter Falstaff, Gadshill, Bardolph, and Peto; Francis following with wine*)

Poins: Welcome, Jack: where hast thou been?

Fal: A plague of all cowards, I say, and a vengeance too! marry, and amen! Give me a cup of sack, boy. . . . A plague of all cowards! Give me a cup of sack, rogue. Is there no virtue extant? (*He drinks*)

Prince: Didst thou never see Titan kiss a dish of butter? . . .

Fal: You rogue, here's lime in this sack too: there is nothing but roguery to be found in villainous man: yet a coward is worse than a cup of sack with lime in it. A villainous coward! Go thy ways, old Jack; die when thou wilt, if manhood, good manhood, be not forgot upon the face of the earth, then am I a shotten herring. There lives not three good men unhanged in England; and one of them is fat, and grows old: God help the while! a bad world, I say. . . . A plague of all cowards, I say still.

Prince: How now, wool-sack! what mutter you?

Fal: A king's son! If I do not beat thee out of thy kingdom with a dagger of lath, and drive all thy subjects afore thee like a flock of wild geese, I'll never wear hair on my face more. You Prince of Wales!

Prince: Why, what's the matter?

Fal: Are not you a coward? answer me to that: and Poins there?

Poins: 'Zounds, ye fat paunch, an ye call me coward, by the Lord, I'll stab thee.

Fal: I call thee coward! I'll see thee damned ere I call thee coward: but I would give a thousand pound I could run as fast as thou canst. You are straight enough in the shoulders, you care not who sees your back: call you that backing of your friends? A plague upon such backing! give me them that will face me. Give me a cup of sack: I am a rogue, if I drunk to-day.

Prince: O villain! thy lips are scarce wiped since thou drunkest last.

Fal: All's one for that. (*He drinks.*) A plague of all cowards, still say I.

Prince: What's the matter?

Fal: What's the matter! there be four of us here have ta'en a thousand pound this day morning.

Prince: Where is it, Jack? where is it?

Fal: Where is it! taken from us it is: a hundred upon poor four of us.

Prince: What, a hundred, man?

Fal: I am a rogue, if I were not at half-sword with a dozen of
them two hours together. I have 'scaped, by miracle. I am
eight times thrust through the doublet, four through the hose;
my buckler cut through and through; my sword hacked like a
hand-saw! I never dealt better since I was a man: all would not
do. A plague of all cowards! Let them speak: if they speak more
or less than truth, they are villains and the sons of darkness.

Prince: Speak, sirs; how was it?

Gads: We four set upon some dozen –

Fal: Sixteen at least, my lord.

Gads: And bound them.

Peto: No, no, they were not bound.

Fal: You rogue, they were bound, every man of them. . . .

Gads: As we were sharing, some six or seven fresh men set upon
us –

Fal: And unbound the rest, and then come in the other.

Prince: What, fought you with them all?

Fal: All! I know not what you call all; but if I fought not with
fifty of them, I am a bunch of radish: if there were not two or
three and fifty upon poor old Jack, then am I no two-legged
creature.

Prince: Pray God you have not murdered some of them.

Fal: Nay, that's past praying for: I have peppered two of them;
two I am sure I have paid, two rogues in buckram suits. I tell
thee what, Hal, if I tell thee a lie, spit in my face, call me horse.
Thou knowest my old ward; here I lay, and thus I bore my
point. Four rogues in buckram let drive at me –

Prince: What, four? thou saidst but two even now.

Fal: Four, Hal; I told thee four.

Poins: Ay, ay, he said four.

Fal: These four came all a-front, and mainly thrust at me. I made
me no more ado but took all their seven points in my target,
thus.

Prince: Seven? why, there were but four even now.

Fal: In buckram?

Poins: Ay, four, in buckram suits.

Fal: Seven, by these hilts, or I am a villain else.

Prince: Prithee, let him alone; we shall have more anon.

Fal: Dost thou hear me, Hal?

Prince: Ay, and mark thee too, Jack.

Fal: Do so, for it is worth the listening to. These nine in buckram that I told thee of, –

Prince: So, two more already.

Fal: Their points being broken –

Poins: Down fell their hose.

Fal: Began to give me ground: but I followed me close, came in foot and hand; and with a thought seven of the eleven I paid.

Prince: O monstrous! eleven buckram men grown out of two!

Fal: But, as the devil would have it, three misbegotten knaves in Kendal green came at my back and let drive at me; for it was so dark, Hal, that thou couldst not see thy hand.

Prince: These lies are like their father that begets them; gross as a mountain, open, palpable. Why, thou clay-brained guts, thou knotty-pated fool, thou obscene, greasy tallow-catch, –

Fal: What, art thou mad? art thou mad? is not the truth the truth?

Prince: Why, how couldst thou know these men in Kendal green, when it was so dark thou couldst not see thy hand? come, tell us your reason: what sayest thou to this?

Fal: 'Sblood, you starveling, you elf-skin, you dried neat's tongue, you stock-fish! O for breath to utter what is like thee! you tailor's yard, you sheath, you bow-case, you vile standing tuck, –

Prince: Well, breathe a while, and then to it again: and when thou hast tired thyself in base comparisons, hear me speak but this.

Poins: Mark, Jack.

Prince: We two saw you four set on four and bound them, and were masters of their wealth. Mark, now, how a plain tale shall put you down. Then did we two set on you four; and, with a word, out-faced you from your prize, and have it; yea, and can show it you here in the house: and, Falstaff, you carried your guts away as nimbly, with as quick dexterity, and roared for mercy, and still run and roared, as ever I heard bull-calf. What a slave art thou, to hack thy sword as thou hast done, and then say it was in fight! What trick canst thou now find to hide thee from this open and apparent shame?

Poins: Come, let's hear, Jack; what trick hast thou now?

Fal: By the Lord, I knew ye as well as he that made ye. Why, hear you, my masters: was it for me to kill the heir-apparent?

should I turn upon the true prince? why, thou knowest I am
as valiant as Hercules: but beware instinct; the lion will not
touch the true prince. Instinct is a great matter; I was now a
coward on instinct. I shall think the better of myself and thee
during my life; I for a valiant lion, and thou for a true prince.
But, by the Lord, lads, I am glad you have the money. Hostess,
cap to the doors: watch to-night, pray tomorrow. Gallants,
lads, boys, hearts of gold, all the titles of good fellowship come
to you! What, shall we be merry? shall we have a play extempore?

William Shakespeare (1564–1616) *Henry IV, Part 1*

CAPTAIN KEARNEY

Frederick Marryat joined the Navy as a midshipman in 1806, when he was fourteen. After service in many parts of the world, he returned to England as a Captain. His experiences, and the places he visited, gave him the material for the many novels he now settled down to write. Mr Midshipman Easy, The Phantom Ship *and* Peter Simple *are the best-known of the thirty-odd stories he produced.*

Captain Kearney certainly dealt in the marvellous to admiration, and really told his stories with such earnestness, that I actually believe that he thought he was telling the truth. Never was there such an instance of confirmed habit. Telling a story of a cutting-out expedition, he said, 'The French captain would have fallen by my hand, but just as I levelled my musket, a ball came, and cut off the cock of the lock, as clean as if it was done with a knife – a very remarkable instance,' observed he.

'Not equal to what occurred in a ship I was in,' replied the first lieutenant, 'when the second lieutenant was grazed by a grape shot, which cut off one of his whiskers, and turning round his head to ascertain what was the matter, another grape shot came and took off the other. Now that's what I call a *close shave*.'

'Yes,' replied Captain Kearney, 'very close, indeed, if it were true; but you'll excuse me, Mr Philpott, but you sometimes tell strange stories. I do not mind it myself, but the example is not good to my young relation here, Mr Simple.'

'Captain Kearney,' replied the first lieutenant, laughing very immoderately, 'do you know what the pot called the kettle?'

'No sir, I do not,' retorted the captain, with offended dignity. 'Mr Simple, will you take a glass of wine?'

I thought that this little *brouillerie* would have checked the captain; it did so, but only for a few minutes, when he again commenced. The first lieutenant observed that it would be necessary to let water into the ship every morning, and pump it out, to avoid the smell of the bilge water. 'There are worse smells than bilge water,' replied the captain. 'What do you think of a whole ship's company being nearly poisoned with otto of roses? Yet that occurred to me when in the Mediterranean. I was off Smyrna, cruising for a French ship, that was to sail to France, with a pasha on board, as an ambassador. I knew she would be a good prize, and was looking sharp out, when one morning we discovered her on the lee bow. We made all sail, but she walked away from us, bearing away gradually till we were both before the wind, and at night we lost sight of her. As I knew that she was bound to Marseilles, I made all sail to fall in with her again. The wind was light and variable; but five days afterwards, as I lay in my cot, just before daylight, I smelt a very strong smell, blowing in at the weather port, and coming down the sky-light which was open; and after sniffing at it two or three times, I knew it to be otto of roses. I sent for the officer of the watch, and asked him if there was any thing in sight. He replied "that there was not;" and I ordered him to sweep the horizon with his glass, and look well out to windward. As the wind freshened, the smell became more powerful. I ordered him to get the royal yards across, and all ready to make sail, for I knew that the Turk must be near us. At daylight, there he was, just three miles a-head in the wind's eye. But although he beat us going free, he was no match for us on a wind, and before noon we had possession of him and all his harem. By-the-bye, I could tell you a good story about the ladies. She was a very valuable prize, and among other things, she had a *puncheon* of otto of roses on board –'

'Whew!' cried the first lieutenant. 'What! a whole puncheon?'

'Yes,' replied the captain, 'a Turkish puncheon – not quite so large, perhaps as ours on board; their weights and measures are different. I took out most of the valuables into the brig I commanded – about 20,000 sequins – carpets – and among the rest, this cask of otto of roses, which we had smelt three miles off. We had it safe on board, when the mate of the hold, not slinging it properly, it fell into the spirit-room with a run, and was stove to pieces. Never was such a scene; my first lieutenant and several men on deck fainted; and the men in the hold were brought up lifeless: it was some time before they were recovered. We let the water into the brig, and pumped it out but nothing would take away the smell, which was so overpowering, that before I could get to Malta I had forty men on the sick list. When I arrived there I turned the mate out of the service for his carelessness. It was not until after having smoked the brig, and finding that of little use, after having sunk her for three weeks, that the smell was at all bearable; but even then, it could never be eradicated and the admiral sent the brig home, and she was sold out of the service. They could do nothing with her at the dock-yards. She was broken up, and bought by the people at Brighton and Tunbridge Wells, who used her timbers for turning fancy articles, which, smelling as they did, so strongly of otto of roses, proved very profitable. Were you ever at Brighton, Mr Simple?'

'Never, sir.'

Just at this moment, the officer of the watch came down to say that there was a very large shark under the counter, and wished to know if the captain had any objection to the officers attempting to catch it?

'By no means,' replied Captain Kearney; 'I hate sharks as I do the devil. I nearly lost £14,000 by one, when I was in the Mediterranean.'

'May I inquire how, Captain Kearney?' said the first lieutenant, with a demure face; 'I'm very anxious to know.'

'Why the story is simply this,' replied the captain. . . .

Frederick Marryat, (1792–1848) *Peter Simple*

THE STRANGE YOUNG GENTLEMAN

Oliver Twist, an orphan, runs away from the brutal coffin-maker to whom he has been apprenticed. Here he meets the Artful Dodger and is taken to the old 'fence', or receiver of stolen goods, who lives on the 'earnings' of boy pickpockets.

'Hullo! my covey, what's the row?'

The boy who addressed this inquiry to the young wayfarer was about his own age, but one of the queerest looking boys that Oliver had ever seen. He was a snub-nosed, flat-browed, common-faced boy enough, and as dirty a juvenile as one would wish to see; but he had about him all the airs and manners of a man. He was short of his age: with rather bow-legs, and little, sharp, ugly eyes. His hat was stuck on the top of his head so lightly that it threatened to fall off every moment – and would have done so, very often, if the wearer had not had a knack of every now and then giving his head a sudden twitch; which brought it back to its old place again. He wore a man's coat, which reached nearly to his heels. He had turned the cuffs back, half-way up his arm, to get his hands out of the sleeves, apparently with the ultimate view of thrusting them into the pockets of his corduroy trousers; for there he kept them. He was, altogether, as roystering and swaggering a young gentleman as ever stood four feet six, or something less, in his bluchers...

'Hullo, my covey, what's the row?' said this strange young gentleman to Oliver.

'I am very hungry and tired,' replied Oliver, the tears standing in his eyes as he spoke. 'I have walked a long way. I have been walking these seven days.'

'Walking for sivin days!' said the young gentleman. 'Oh, I see. Beak's order, eh? But,' he added, noticing Oliver's look of surprise, 'I suppose you don't know what a beak is, my flash com-pan-i-on.'

Oliver mildly replied that he had always heard a bird's mouth described by the term in question.

'My eyes, how green!' exclaimed the young gentleman. 'Why, a beak's a madgst'rate; and when you walk by a break's order, it's not straight forerd, but always agoing up and nivir acoming down agin. Was you never on the mill?'

'What mill?' inquired Oliver.

'What mill! – why, *the* mill – the mill as takes up so little room that it'll work inside a Stone Jug; and always goes better when the wind's low with people, than when it's high; acos then they can't get workmen. But come,' said the young gentleman; 'you want grub, and you shall have it. I'm at low-water-mark myself – only one bob and a magpie; but, *as* far *as* it goes, I'll fork out and stump. Up with you on your pins. There! Now then! Morrice!'

Assisting Oliver to rise, the young gentleman took him to an adjacent chandler's shop, where he purchased a sufficiency of ready-dressed ham and a half-quartern loaf, or, as he himself expressed it, 'a fourpenny bran'; the ham, being kept clean and preserved from dust, by the ingenious expedient of making a hole in the loaf by pulling out a portion of the crumb, and stuffing it herein. Taking the bread under his arm, the young gentleman turned into a small public-house, and led the way to a tap-room in the rear of the premises. Here a pot of beer was brought in, by direction of the mysterious youth; and Oliver, falling to, at his new friend's bidding, made a long and hearty meal, during the progress of which the strange boy eyed him from time to time with great attention.

'Going to London?' said the strange boy, when Oliver had at length concluded.

'Yes.'

'Got any lodgings?'

'No.'

'Money?'

'No.'

The strange boy whistled; and put his arms into his pockets as far as the big coat sleeves would let them go.

'Do you live in London?' inquired Oliver.

'Yes. I do, when I'm at home,' replied the boy. 'I suppose you want some place to sleep in to-night, don't you?'

'I do indeed,' answered Oliver. 'I have not slept under a roof since I left the country.'

'Don't fret your eyelids on that score,' said the young gentleman. 'I've got to be in London to-night; and I know a 'spectable old genelman as lives there, wot'll give you lodgings for nothink, and never ask for the change – that is, if any genelman he knows interduces you. And don't he know me? Oh, no! Not in the least! By no means. Certainly not!'

The young gentleman smiled, as if to intimate that the latter fragments of discourse were playfully ironical; and finished the beer as he did so.

This unexpected offer of shelter was too tempting to be resisted; especially as it was immediately followed up by the assurance, that the old gentleman already referred to would doubtless provide Oliver with a comfortable place without loss of time. This led to a more friendly and confidential dialogue; from which Oliver discovered that his friend's name was Jack Dawkins, and that he was a peculiar pet and *protégé* of the elderly gentleman before mentioned.

Mr Dawkin's appearance did not say a vast deal in favour of the comforts which his patron's interest obtained for those whom he took under his protection; but, as he had a rather flighty and dissolute mode of conversing, and furthermore avowed that among his intimate friends he was better known by the *sobriquet* of 'The artful Dodger,' Oliver concluded that, being of a dissipated and careless turn, the moral precepts of his benefactor had hitherto been thrown away upon him. Under this impression, he secretly resolved to cultivate the good opinion of the old gentleman as quickly as possible; and, if he found the Dodger incorrigible, as he more than half suspected he should, to decline the honour of his farther acquaintance.

As John Dawkins objected to their entering London before nightfall, it was nearly eleven o'clock when they reached the turnpike at Islington. They crossed from the Angel into St. John's-road, struck down the small street which terminates at Sadler's Wells Theatre, through the workhouse, across the classic ground which once bore the name of Hockley-in-the-Hole, thence into Little Saffron-hill, and so into Saffron-hill the Great, along which the Dodger scudded at a rapid pace, directing Oliver to follow close at his heels.

Although Oliver had enough to occupy his attention in keeping sight of his leader, he could not help bestowing a few hasty glances on either side of the way as he passed along. A dirtier or more wretched place he had never seen. The street was very narrow and muddy, and the air was impregnated with filthy odours. There were a good many small shops; but the only stock in trade appeared to be heaps of children, who, even at that time of night, were crawling in and out at the doors, or screaming from the inside. The sole places that seemed to prosper, amid the general blight of the place, were the public-houses; and in them the lowest orders of Irish were wrangling with might and main. Covered ways and yards, which here and there diverged from the main street, disclosed little knots of houses where drunken men and women were positively wallowing in filth; and from several of the door-ways, great ill-looking fellows were cautiously emerging, bound, to all appearance, on no very well-disposed or harmless errands.

Oliver was just considering whether he hadn't better run away, when they reached the bottom of the hill. His conductor, catching him by the arm, pushed open the door of a house near Field-lane, and, drawing him into the passage, closed it behind them.

'Now, then!' cried a voice from below, in reply to a whistle from the Dodger.

'Plummy and slam!' was the reply.

This seemed to be some watchword or signal that all was right; for the light of a feeble candle gleamed on the wall at the remote end of the passage, and a man's face peeped out from where a balustrade of the old kitchen staircase had been broken away.

'There's two on you,' said the man, thrusting the candle farther out, and shading his eyes with his hand. 'Who's the t'other one?'

'A new pal,' replied Jack Dawkins, pulling Oliver forward.

'Where did he come from?'

'Greenland. Is Fagin up stairs?'

'Yes, he's a sortin' the wipes. Up with you!' The candle was drawn back, and the face disappeared.

Oliver, groping his way with one hand, and having the other firmly grasped by his companion, ascended with much difficulty the dark and broken stairs, which his conductor mounted with an ease and expedition that showed he was well acquainted with them. He threw open the door of a back room, and drew Oliver in after him.

The walls and ceiling of the room were perfectly black with age and dirt. There was a deal table before the fire, upon which were a candle stuck in a ginger-beer bottle, two or three pewter pots, a loaf and butter, and a plate. In a frying-pan, which was on the fire, and which was secured to the mantelshelf by a string, some sausages were cooking; and standing over them, with a toasting-fork in his hand, was a very old shrivelled Jew, whose villainous-looking and repulsive face was obscured by a quantity of matted red hair. He was dressed in a greasy flannel gown, with his throat bare; and seemed to be diving his attention between the frying-pan and a clothes-horse, over which a great number of silk handkerchiefs were hanging. Several rough beds, made of old sacks, were huddled side by side on the floor. Seated round the table were four or five boys, none older than the Dodger, smoking long clay pipes, and drinking spirits with the air of middle-aged men. These all crowded about their associate as he whispered a few words to the Jew, and then turned round and grinned at Oliver. So did the Jew himself, toasting-fork in hand.

'This is him, Fagin,' said Jack Dawkins; 'my friend Oliver Twist.'

The Jew grinned; and, making a low obeisance to Oliver, took him by the hand, and hoped he should have the honour of his intimate acquaintance. Upon this the young gentlemen with the pipes came round him, and shook both his hands very hard – especially the one in which he held his little bundle. One young gentleman was very anxious to hang up his cap for him; and another was so obliging as to put his hands in his pockets, in order that, as he was very tired, he might not have the trouble of emptying them himself when he went to bed. These civilities would probably have been extended much farther, but for a liberal exercise of the Jew's toasting-fork on the heads and shoulders of the affectionate youths who offered them.

'We are very glad to see you, Oliver – very,' said the Jew. 'Dodger, take off the sausages, and draw a tub near the fire for Oliver. Ah, you're a-staring at the pocket-handkerchiefs! eh, my dear! There are a good many of 'em, ain't there? We've just looked 'em out, ready for the wash; that's all, Oliver; that's all. Ha! ha! ha!'

The latter part of his speech was hailed by a boisterous shout from all the hopeful pupils of the merry old gentleman, in the midst of which they went to supper.

Oliver ate his share, and the Jew then mixed him a glass of hot gin and water, telling him he must drink it off directly, because another gentleman wanted the tumbler. Oliver did as he was desired. Immediately afterwards he felt himself gently lifted on to one of the sacks, and then he sank into a deep sleep.

Charles Dickens (1812–1870), *Oliver Twist*

THE NAVY OUTWITTED

Jim Davis (in John Masefield's novel) is a boy of twelve who is kidnapped by a gang of smugglers because he knows too much about them. Here, as they are making for France, they are detected by a customs cutter (a single-masted vessel) which tries to chase them within reach of three frigates – heavy-armed warships next in size to battleships.

By this time the other smugglers had become alarmed. The longboat gun, which worked on a slide abaft all, was cleared, and the two little cohorns, or hand-swivel guns, which pointed over the sides, were trained and loaded. A man swarmed up the main-mast to look around. 'The cutter's bearing up to close,' he called out. 'I see she's the Salcombe boat.'

'That shows they have information,' said Marah grimly, 'otherwise they'd not be looking for us here. Someone has been talking to his wife.' He hailed the masthead again. 'Have the frigates seen us yet?'

For answer, the man took a hurried glance to windward, turned visibly white to the lips, and slid down a rope to the deck. 'Bearing down fast, under stunsails,' he reported. 'The cutter's signalled them with her top-sail. There's three frigates coming down,' he added.

'Right,' said Marah. 'I'll go up and see for myself.'

He went up, and came down again looking very ugly. He evidently thought that he was in a hole. 'As she goes,' he called to the helmsman, 'get all you can on the sheets, boys. Now, Jim, you're up a tree; you're within an hour of being pressed into the Navy. How'd ye like to be a ship's boy, hey, and get tickled up by a bo'sun's rope-end?'

'I shouldn't like it at all,' I answered.

'You'll like it a jolly sight less than that,' said he, 'and it's what you'll probably be. We're ten miles from home. The cutter's in the road. The frigates will be on us in half an hour.

124

It will be a mighty close call, my son; we shall have to fight to get clear.'

At that instant of time something went overhead with a curious whanging whine.

'That's a three-pound ball,' said Marah, pointing to a spurt upon a wave. 'The cutter wants us to stop and have breakfast with 'em.'

'Whang,' went another shot, flying far overhead. 'Fire away,' said Marah. 'You're more than a mile away; you will not hit us at that range.'

He shifted his course a little, edging more towards the shore, so as to cut transversely across the cutter's bows. We ran for twenty minutes in the course of the frigates; by that time the cutter was within half a mile and the frigates within three miles of us. All the cutter's guns were peppering at us, a shot or two went through our sails, one shot knocked a splinter from our fife-rail.

'They shoot a treat, don't they?' said Marah. 'Another minute and they will be knocking away a spar.'

Just as he spoke, there came another shot from the cutter; something aloft went 'crack'; a rope unreeved from its pulley and rattled on to the deck; the mizen came down in a heap: the halliards had been cut clean through. The men leaped to repair the damage; it took but a minute or two, but we had lost way; the next shot took us square amidships and tore off a yard of our lee side.

'We must give them one in return,' he said. 'Aft to the gun, boys.'

The men trained the long gun on the cutter. 'Oh, Marah,' I said, 'don't fire on Englishmen.'

'Who began the firing?' he answered. 'I'm going to knock away some of their sails. Stand clear of the breach,' he shouted, as he pulled the trigger-string.

The gun roared and recoiled; a hole appeared as if by magic in the swelling square foresail of the cutter. 'Load with bar-shot and chain,' said Marah. 'Another like that and we shall rip the whole sail off. Mind your eye. There goes her gun again.'

This time the shot struck the sea beside us, sending a spout of water over our rail. Again Marah pulled his trigger-string, the gun fell over on its side, and the cutter's mast seemed to collapse into itself as though it were wrapping itself up in its own canvas. A huge loose clue of sail – the foresail's starboard leach – flew up into the air; the boom swung after it; the gaff toppled over from above; we saw the topmast dive like a lunging rapier into the sea. We had torn the foresail in two, and the shot passing on had smashed the foremast just below the cap. All her sails lay in a confused heap just forward of the mast.

'That's done her,' said one of the smugglers. 'She can't even use her gun now.'

'Hooray!' cried another. 'We're the boys for a lark.'

'Are you?' said Marah. 'We got the frigates to clear yet, my son. They'll be in range in two minutes or less. Look at them.'

Tearing after us, in chase, under all sail, came the frigates. Their bows were burrowing into white heaps of foam; we could see the red portlids and the shining gun-muzzles; we could see the scarlet coats of the marines, and the glint of brass on the poops. A flame spurted from the bows of the leader. She was firing a shot over us to bid us heave to. The smugglers looked at each other; they felt that the game was up. Bang! Another shot splashed into the sea beside us, and bounded on from wave to wave, sending up huge splashes at each bound. A third shot came from the second frigate, but this also missed. Marah was leaning over our lee rail, looking at the coast of France, still several miles away. 'White water,' he cried suddenly. 'Here's the Green Stones. We shall do them yet.'

I could see no green stones, but a quarter of a mile away, on our port-hand, the sea was all a cream of foam above reefs and sands just covered by the tide. If they were to help us, it was none too soon, for by this time the leading frigate was only a hundred yards from us. Her vast masts towered over us. I could look into her open bow ports; I could see the men at the bow guns waiting for the word to fire. I have often seen ships since then, but I never saw any ship so splendid and so terrible as that one. She was the Laocoòn, and her figurehead was twined with serpents. The line of her ports was of a dull yellow colour, and as all her ports were open, the portlids made scarlet marks all along it. Her great lower studding sail swept out from her side for all the world like a butterfly-net, raking the top of the sea for us. An officer stood on the forecastle with a speaking-trumpet in his hand.

'Stand by!' cried Marah. 'They're going to hail us.'

'Ahoy, the lugger there!' yelled the officer. 'Heave to at once or I sink you. Heave to.'

'Answer him in French,' said Marah to one of the men.

A man made some answer in French; I think he said he didn't understand. The officer told a marine to fire at us. The bullet whipped through the mizen. 'Bang' went one of the main-deck guns just over our heads. We felt a rush and shock, and our mizen mast and sail went over the side.

Marah stood up and raised his hand. 'We surrender, sir!' he shouted. 'We surrender! Down helm, boys.'

We swung round on our keel, and came to the wind. We saw the officer nod approval and speak a word to the sailing-master, and then the great ship lashed past us, a mighty, straining, heaving fabric of beauty, whose lower studding sails were half-way to their irons.

'Now for it!' said Marah. He hauled his wind, and the lugger shot off towards the broken water. 'If we get among those shoals,' he said, 'we're safe as houses. The frigate's done. She's going at such a pace they will never stop her. Not till she's gone a mile. Not without they rip the masts out of her. That officer ought to have known that trick. That will be a lesson to you, Mr Jim. If ever you're in a little ship, and you get chased by a big ship, you keep on till she's right on top of you, and then luff hard all you know, and the chances are you'll get a mile start before they come round to go after you.'

We had, in fact, doubled like a hare, and the frigate, like a greyhound, had torn on ahead, unable to turn. We saw her lower stunsail boom carry away as they took in the sail, and we could see her seamen running to their quarters ready to brace the yards and bring the ship to her new course. The lugger soon gathered way and tore on, but it was now blowing very fresh indeed, and the sea before us was one lashing smother of breakers. Marah seemed to think nothing of that; he was watching the frigates. One, a slower sailor than the other, was sailing back to the fleet; the second had hove to about a mile away, with her longboat lowered to pursue us. The boat was just clear of her shadow; crowding all sail in order to get us. The third ship, the ship which we had tricked, was hauling to the wind, with her light canvas clued up for furling. In a few moments she was braced up and standing towards us but distant about a mile.

Suddenly both frigates opened fire, and the great cannon balls ripped up the sea all round us.

'They'll sink us, sure,' said one of the smugglers with a grin.

The men all laughed, and I laughed too; we were all so very much interested in what was going to happen. The guns fired steadily one after the other in a long rolling roar. The men laughed at each shot.

'They couldn't hit the sea,' they said derisively. 'The navy gunners are no use at all.'

'No,' said Marah, 'they're not. But if they keep their course another half-minute they'll be on the sunk reef, and a lot of 'em'll be drowned. I wonder will the old Laocoòn take a hint.'

'Give 'em the pennant,' said Gateo.

'Ay, give it 'em,' said half a dozen others. 'Don't let 'em wreck.'

Marah opened the flag-locker, and took out a blue pennant (it had a white ball in the middle of it), which he hoisted to his main truck. 'Let her go off,' he cried to the helmsman.

For just a moment we lay broadside on to the frigate, a fair target for her guns, so that she could see the pennant blowing out clear.

'You see, Jim?' asked Marah. 'That pennant means "You are standing in to danger." Now we will luff again.'

'I don't think they saw it, guv'nor,' said one of the sailors as another shot flew over us. 'They'll have to send below to get their glasses, those blind navy jokers.'

'Off,' said Marah, quickly; and again we lay broadside on, tumbling in the swell, shipping heavy sprays.

This time they saw it, for the Laocoòn's helm was put down, her great sails shivered and threshed, and she stood off on the other tack. As she stood away we saw an officer leap on to the taffrail, holding on by the mizen backstays.

'Tar my wig,' said Marah, 'if he isn't bowing to us!'

Sure enough the officer took off his hat to us and bowed gracefully.

'Polite young man,' said Marah. 'We will give them the other pennant.'

Another flag, a red pennant, was hoisted in place of the blue.

'Wishing you a pleasant voyage,' said Marah. 'Now luff, my sons. That longboat will be on to us.'

Indeed, the longboat had crept to within six hundred yards of us; it was time we were moving, though the guns were no longer on us from the ships.

'Mind your helm, boys,' said Marah as he went forward to the bows. 'I've got to con you through a lot of bad rocks. You'll have to steer small or die.'

John Masefield (1878–1967), *Jim Davis*

THE NIGHT THE GHOST GOT IN

James Thurber was an American cartoonist and writer of humorous books and plays, who spent most of his life in journalism.

The ghost that got into our house on the night of November 17, 1915, raised such a hullabaloo of misunderstandings that I am sorry I didn't just let it keep on walking, and go to bed. Its advent caused my mother to throw a shoe through a window of the house next door and ended up with my grandfather shooting a patrolman. I am sorry, therefore, as I have said, that I ever paid any attention to the footsteps.

They began about a quarter past one o'clock in the morning, a rhythmic, quick-cadenced walking around the dining-room table. My mother was asleep in one room upstairs, my brother Herman in another; grandfather was in the attic, in the old walnut bed which, as you will remember, once fell on my father. I had just stepped out of the bathtub and was busily rubbing myself with a towel when I heard the steps. They were the steps of a man walking rapidly around the dining-room table downstairs. The light from the bathroom shone down the back steps, which dropped directly into the dining-room; I could see the faint shine of plates on the plate-rail; I couldn't see the table. The steps kept going round and round the table; at regular intervals a board creaked, when it was trod upon. I supposed at first that it was my father or my brother Roy, who had gone to Indianapolis but were expected home at any time. I suspected next that it was a burglar. It did not enter my mind until later that it was a ghost.

After the walking had gone on for perhaps three minutes, I tiptoed to Herman's room. 'Psst!' I hissed in the dark, shaking him. 'Awp,' he said, in the low, hopeless tone of a despondent beagle – he always half suspected that something would 'get him' in the night. I told him who I was. 'There's something downstairs!' I said. He got up and followed me to the head of the back staircase. We listened together. There was no sound. The steps had ceased.

Herman looked at me in some alarm: I had only the bath towel around my waist. He wanted to go back to bed, but I gripped his arm. 'There's something down there!' I said. Instantly the steps began again, circled the dining-room table like a man running, and started up the stairs towards us, heavily, two at a time. The light still shone palely down the stairs; we saw nothing coming; we only heard the steps. Herman rushed to his room and slammed the door. I slammed shut the door at the stairs top and held my knee against it. After a long minute, I slowly opened it again. There was nothing there. There was no sound. None of us ever heard the ghost again.

The slamming of the doors had aroused mother: she peered out of her room. 'What on earth are you boys doing?' she demanded. Herman ventured out of his room. 'Nothing,' he said, gruffly, but he was, in color, a light green. 'What was all that running around downstairs?' said mother. So she had heard the steps, too! We just looked at her. 'Burglars!' she shouted intuitively. I tried to quiet her by starting lightly downstairs.

'Come on, Herman,' I said.

'I'll stay with mother,' he said. 'She's all excited.'

I stepped back onto the landing.

'Don't either of you go a step,' said mother. 'We'll call the police.' Since the phone was downstairs, I didn't see how we were going to call the police – nor did I want the police – but mother made one of her quick, incomparable decisions. She flung up a window of her bedroom which faced the bedroom windows of the house of a neighbor, picked up a shoe, and whammed it through a pane of glass across the narrow space that separated the two houses. Glass tinkled into the bedroom occupied by a retired engraver named Bodwell and his wife. Bodwell had been for some years in rather a bad way and was subject to mild 'attacks'. Most everybody we knew or lived near had *some* kind of attacks.

It was now about two o'clock of a moonless night; clouds hung black and low. Bodwell was at the window in a minute, shouting, frothing a little, shaking his fist. 'We'll sell the house and go back to Peoria,' we could hear Mrs Bodwell saying. It was some time before mother 'got through' to Bodwell. 'Burglars!' she shouted. 'Burglars in the house!' Herman and I hadn't dared to tell her that it was not burglars but ghosts, for she was even more afraid of ghosts than of burglars. Bodwell at first thought that she meant there were burglars in his house, but finally he quieted down and called the police for us over an extension phone by his bed. After he had disappeared from the window, mother suddenly made as if to throw another shoe, not because there was further need of it but, as she later explained, because the thrill of heaving a shoe through a window glass had enormously taken her fancy. I prevented her.

The police were on hand in a commendably short time: a Ford sedan full of them, two on motorcycles, and a patrol wagon with about eight in it and a few reporters. They began banging at our front door. Flashlights shot streaks of gleam up and down the walls, across the yard, down the walk between our house and Bodwell's. 'Open up!' cried a hoarse voice. 'We're men from Headquarters!' I wanted to go down and let them in, since there they were, but mother wouldn't hear of it. 'You haven't a stitch on,' she pointed out. 'You'd catch your death.' I wound the towel around me again. Finally the cops put their shoulders to our big heavy front door with its thick beveled glass and broke it in: I could hear a rending of wood and a splash of glass on the floor of the hall. Their lights played all over the living-room and criss-crossed nervously in the dining-room, stabbed into hallways, shot up the front stairs and finally up the back. They caught me standing in my towel at the top. A heavy policeman bounded up the steps. 'Who are you?' he demanded. 'I live here,' I said. 'Well, whattsa matta, ya hot?' he asked. It was, as a matter of fact, cold; I went to my room and pulled on some trousers. On my way out, a cop stuck a gun into my ribs. 'Whatta you doin' here?' he demanded. 'I live here,' I said.

The officer in charge reported to mother. 'No sign of nobody, lady,' he said. 'Musta got away – whatt'd he look like?' 'There were two or three of them,' mother said, 'whooping and carrying on and slamming doors.' 'Funny,' said the cop. 'All ya windows and doors was locked on the inside right as a tick.'

Downstairs, we could hear the tromping of the other police. Police were all over the place; doors were yanked open, drawers were yanked open, windows were shot up and pulled down, furniture fell with dull thumps. A half-dozen policemen emerged out of the darkness of the front hallway upstairs. They began to ransack the floor: pulled beds away from walls, tore clothes off hooks in the closets, pulled suitcases and boxes off shelves. One

of them found an old zither than Roy had won in a pool tourna-
ment. 'Looky here, Joe,' he said strumming it with a big paw.
The cop named Joe took it and turned it over. 'What is it?' he
asked me. 'It's an old zither our guinea pig used to sleep on,' I
said. It was true that a pet guinea pig we once had would never
sleep anywhere except on the zither but I should never have said
so. Joe and the other cop looked at me a long time. They put the
zither back on a shelf.

'No sign o' nuthin',' said the cop who had first spoken to
mother. 'This guy,' he explained to the others, jerking a thumb
at me, 'was nekked. The lady seems historical.' They all nodded,
but said nothing; just looked at me. In the small silence we all
heard a creaking in the attic. Grandfather was turning over in bed.
'What's 'at?' snapped Joe. Five or six cops sprang for the attic
door before I could intervene or explain. I realized that it would
be bad if they burst in on grandfather unannounced, or even
announced. He was going through a phase in which he believed
that General Meade's men, under steady hammering by Stone-
wall Jackson, were beginning to retreat and even desert.

When I got to the attic, things were pretty confused. Grandfather had evidently jumped to the conclusion that the police
were deserters from Meade's army, trying to hide away in his
attic. He bounded out of bed wearing a long flannel nightgown
over long woolen underwear, a nightcap, and a leather jacket
around his chest. The cops must have realized at once that the
indignant white-haired old man belonged in the house, but they
had no chance to say so. 'Back, ye cowardly dogs!' roared grandfather. 'Back t' the lines, ye goddam lily-livered cattle!' With that,
he fetched the officer who found the zither a flat-handed smack
alongside his head that sent him sprawling. The others beat a
retreat, but not fast enough; grandfather grabbed Zither's gun
from its holster and let fly. The report seemed to crack the rafters;
smoke filled the attic. A cop cursed and shot his hand to his
shoulder. Somehow, we all finally got downstairs again and
locked the door against the old gentleman. He fired once or twice
more in the darkness and then went back to bed. 'That was grandfather,' I explained to Joe, out of breath. 'He thinks you're
deserters.' 'I'll say he does,' said Joe.

The cops were reluctant to leave without getting their hands on
somebody besides grandfather; the night had been distinctly a

defeat for them. Furthermore, they obviously didn't like the 'layout'; something looked – and I can see their viewpoint – phony. They began to poke into things again. A reporter, a thin-faced, wispy man, came up to me. I had put on one of mother's blouses, not being able to find anything else. The reporter looked at me with mingled suspicion and interest. 'Just what the hell is the real lowdown here, Bud?' he asked. I decided to be frank with him. 'We had ghosts,' I said. He gazed at me a long time as if I were a slot machine into which he had, without results, dropped a nickel. Then he walked away. The cops followed him, the one grandfather shot holding his now-bandaged arm, cursing and blaspheming. 'I'm gonna get my gun back from that old bird,' said the zither-cop. 'Yeh,' said Joe. 'You – and who else?' I told them I would bring it to the station house next day.

'What was the matter with that one policeman?' mother asked, after they had gone. 'Grandfather shot him,' I said. 'What for?' she demanded. I told her he was a deserter. 'Of all things!' said mother. 'He was such a nice-looking young man.'

Grandfather was fresh as a daisy and full of jokes at breakfast next morning. We thought at first he had forgotten all about what had happened, but he hadn't. Over his third cup of coffee, he glared at Herman and me. 'What was the idee of all them cops tarryhootin' round the house last night?' he demanded. He had us there.

James Thurber (1894–1961), *The Thurber Carnival*

5

BOYS AND MEN

THE SANDHILL SCHOOL

William Cobbett, the son of a small farmer, lived at the beginning of the last century. After being a farm labourer, a clerk and a soldier he settled down to writing.

There is a place called the Bourne, which lies in the heath at about a mile from Farnham. It is a winding narrow valley, down which, during the wet season of the year, there runs a stream beginning at the Holt Forest, and emptying itself into the Wey just below Moor Park, which was the seat of Sir William Temple, when Swift was residing with him. There is a little hop-garden in which I used to work from eight to ten years old; from which I have scores of times run in order to follow the hounds, leaving the hoe to do the best that it could to destroy the weeds; but the most interesting thing was a sandhill, which goes from a part of the heath down to the rivulet.

As a due mixture of pleasure with toil, I with my two brothers, used occasionally to disport ourselves, as the lawyers call it, at this sandhill. Our diversion was this: one used to draw his arms out of the sleeves of his smock-frock, and lay himself down with his arms by his sides; and then the others, one at head and the other at feet, sent him rolling down the hill like a barrel or a log of wood. By the time he got to the bottom, his hair, eyes, ears, nose and mouth, were all full of this loose sand; then the others took their turn, and at every roll, there was a monstrous spell of laughter. I often told my sons of this while they were very little, and (in 1822) I took one of them to see the spot. But that was not all. This was the spot where I was receiving my education; and this was the sort of education; and I am perfectly satisfied that if I had not received such an education, or something very much like it; that, if I had been brought up a milksop, with a nurserymaid everlastingly at my heels, I should have been at this day as great a fool, as inefficient a mortal, as any of those frivolous idiots that are turned out from Winchester or Westminster School or from any of those dens of dunces called Colleges and Universities. It is impossible to say how much I owe to that sandhill; and I went to return it my thanks.

At eleven years of age my employment was clipping of box-edgings and weeding beds of flowers in the garden of the Bishop of Winchester, at the Castle of Farnham. I had always been fond of beautiful gardens; and, a gardener, who had just come from the King's gardens at Kew, gave such a description of them as made me instantly resolve to work in these gardens. The next morning without saying a word to anybody, off I set, with no clothes, except those upon my back, and thirteen halfpence in my pocket. I found that I must go to Richmond, and I, accordingly, went on, from place to place, inquiring my way thither. A long day (it was in June) brought me to Richmond in the afternoon. Two pennyworth of bread and cheese and a pennyworth of small beer, which I had on the road, and one halfpenny that I had lost somehow or other, left three pence in my pocket. With this for my whole fortune, I was trudging through Richmond in my blue-smock frock and my red garters tied under my knees, when, staring about me, my eye fell upon a little book, in a bookseller's window: 'Tale of a Tub; price 3d.' The title was so odd, that my curiosity was excited. I had the 3d., but, then, I could have no supper. In I went and got the little book, which I was so impatient to read, that I got over into a field, at the upper corner of Kew Gardens, where there stood a haystack. On the shady side of this, I sat down to read. The book was so different from anything that I had ever read before: it was something so new to my mind, that, though I could not at all understand some of it, it delighted me beyond description; and it produced what I have always con-sidered a sort of birth of intellect. I read on till it was dark, with-out any thought about supper or bed. When I could see no longer, I put my little book in my pocket, and tumbled down by the side of the stack, where I slept till the birds in Kew Garden awaked me in the morning; when off I started to Kew, reading my little book. The singularity of my dress, the simplicity of my manner, my confident and lively air, induced the gardener, who was a Scotchman, I remember, to give me victuals, find my lodging, and set me to work. And, it was during the period that I was at Kew, that the King and two of his brothers laughed at the oddness of my dress, while I was sweeping the grass plat round the foot of the Pagoda. The gardener, seeing me fond of books, lent me some gardening books to read; but, these I could not relish after my Tale of a Tub, which I carried about with me wherever I went, and when I, at about twenty years old, lost it in a box that fell overboard in the Bay of Funday in North America, the loss gave me greater pain that I have ever felt at losing thousands of pounds.

William Cobbett (1762–1835), *The Progress of a Ploughboy*
(ed. Reitzel)

DAVID'S JOURNEY TO LONDON

David Copperfield was the only child of a young widow, who had a servant called Peggotty. On returning from a holiday at Yarmouth with Peggotty's brother, Ham, David found that his mother had remarried. David's new father, a man called Murdstone, and his sister Miss Murdstone treated him brutally, and decided that he should be sent to school near London. He travelled by stage-coach, on his own.

The coach was in the yard, shining very much all over, but without any horses to it as yet; and it looked in that state as of nothing was more unlikely than its ever going to London. I was thinking this, and wondering what would ultimately become of my box, which Mr Barkis had put down on the yard-pavement by the pole (he having driven up the yard to turn his cart), and also what would ultimately become of me, when a lady looked out of a bow-window where some fowls and joints of meat were hanging up, and said –

'Is that the little gentleman from Blunderstone?'

'Yes, Ma'am,' I said.

'What name?' inquired the lady.

'Copperfield, Ma'am,' I said.

'That won't do,' returned the lady. 'Nobody's dinner is paid for here, in that name.·

'Is it Murdstone, Ma'am?' I said.

'If you're Master Murdstone,' said the lady, 'why do you go and give another name first?'

I explained to the lady how it was, who then rang a bell and called out, 'William! show the coffee-room!' upon which a waiter came running out of a kitchen on the opposite side of the yard to show it, and seemed a good deal surprised when he found he was only to show it to me.

It was a large long room with some large maps in it. I doubt if I could have felt much stranger if the maps had been real foreign countries, and I cast away in the middle of them. I felt it was taking a liberty to sit down, with my cap in my hand, on the corner of the chair nearest the door; and when the waiter laid a cloth on purpose for me, and put a set of castors on it, I think I must have turned red all over with modesty.

He brought me some chops and vegetables, and took the covers off in such a bouncing manner that I was afraid I must have given him some offence. But he greatly relieved my mind by putting a chair for me at the table, and saying, very affably, 'Now, six-foot! come on!'

I thanked him, and took my seat at the board; but found it extremely difficult to handle my knife and fork with anything like dexterity, or to avoid splashing myself with the gravy, while he was standing opposite, staring so hard, and making me blush in the most dreadful manner every time I caught his eye. After watching me into the second chop, he said, 'There's half a pint of ale for you. Will you have it now?'

I thanked him and said 'Yes.' Upon which he poured it out of a jug into a large tumbler, and held it up against the light, and made it look beautiful.

'My eye!' he said. 'It seems a good deal, don't it?'

'It does seem a good deal,' I answered, with a smile. For it was quite delightful to me to find him so pleasant. He was twinkling-eyed, pimple-faced man, with his hair standing upright all over his head; and as he stood with one arm a-kimbo, holding up the glass to the light with the other hand, he looked quite friendly.

'There was a gentleman here yesterday,' he said – 'a stout gentleman, by the name of Topsawyer – perhaps you know him?'

'No,' I said, 'I don't think –'

'In breeches and gaiters, broad-brimmed hat, gray coat, speckled choker,' said the waiter.

'No,' I said, bashfully, 'I haven't the pleasure –'

'He came in here,' said the waiter, looking at the light through the tumbler, 'ordered a glass of this ale – *would* order it – I told him not – drank it, and fell dead. It was too old for him. It oughtn't to be drawn; that's the fact.'

I was very much shocked to hear of this melancholy accident, and said I thought I had better have some water.

'Why, you see,' said the waiter, still looking at the light through the tumbler, with one of his eyes shut up, 'our people don't like things being ordered and left. It offends 'em. But *I*'ll drink it, if you like. I am used to it, and use is everything. I don't think it'll hurt me, if I throw my head back, and take it off quick. Shall I?'

I replied that he would much oblige me by drinking it, if he thought he could do it safely, but by no means otherwise. When he did throw his head back, and take it off quick, I had a horrible fear, I confess, of seeing him meet the fate of the lamented Mr Topsawyer, and fall lifeless on the carpet. But it didn't hurt him. On the contrary, I thought he seemed the fresher for it.

'What have we got here?' he said, putting a fork into my dish. 'Not chops?'

'Chops,' I said.

'Lord bless my soul!' he exclaimed, 'I didn't know they were chops. Why, a chop's the very thing to take off the bad effects of that beer! Ain't it lucky!'

So he took a chop by the bone in one hand, and a potato in the other, and ate away with a very good appetite, to my extreme satisfaction. He afterwards took another chop, and another potato; and after that another chop and another potato. When we had done, he brought me a pudding, and having set it before me, seemed to ruminate, and to become absent in his mind for some moments.

'How's the pie?' he said, rousing himself.

'It's a pudding,' I made answer.

'Pudding!' he exclaimed. 'Why, bless me, so it is! What!' looking at it nearer. 'You don't mean to say it's a batter-pudding?'

'Yes, it is indeed.'

'Why, a batter-pudding,' he said, taking up a table-spoon, 'is my favourite pudding! Ain't that lucky? Come on, little un', and let's see who'll get most.'

The waiter certainly got most. He entreated me more than once to come in and win, but what with his table-spoon to my tea-spoon, his dispatch to my dispatch, and his appetite to my appetite, I was left far behind at the first mouthful, and had no chance with him. I never saw any one enjoy a pudding so much, I think; and he laughed, when it was all gone, as if his enjoyment of it lasted still.

Finding him so very friendly and companionable, it was then that I asked for the pen and ink and paper, to write to Peggotty. He not only brought it immediately, but was good enough to look over me while I wrote the letter. When I had finished it, he asked me where I was going to school.

I said, 'Near London,' which was all I knew.

'Oh, my eye!' he said, looking very low-spirited, 'I am sorry for that.'

'Why?' I asked him.

'Oh Lord!' he said, shaking his head, 'that's the school where they broke the boy's ribs – two ribs – a little boy he was. I should say he was – let me see – how old are you, about?'

I told him between eight and nine.

'That's just his age,' he said. 'He was eight years and six months old when they broke his first rib; eight years and eight months old when they broke his second, and did for him.'

I could not disguise from myself, or from the waiter, that this was an uncomfortable coincidence, and inquired how it was done. His answer was not cheering to my spirits, for it consisted of two dismal words, 'with whopping.'

The blowing of the coach-horn in the yard was a seasonable diversion, which made me get up and hesitatingly inquire, in the mingled pride and diffidence of having a purse (which I took out of my pocket), if there were anything to pay.

'There's a sheet of letter-paper,' he returned. 'Did you ever buy a sheet of letter-paper?'

I could not remember that I ever had.

'It's dear,' he said, 'on account of the duty. Threepence. That's the way we're taxed in this country. There's nothing else, except the waiter. Never mind the ink. *I* lose by that.'

'What should you – what should I – how much ought I to – what would it be right to pay the waiter, if you please?' I stammered, blushing.

'If I hadn't a family, and that family hadn't the cowpock,' said the waiter, 'I wouldn't take a sixpence. If I didn't support a aged pairint, and a lovely sister,' here the waiter was greatly agitated – 'I wouldn't take a farthing. If I had a good place, and was treated well here, I should beg acceptance of a trifle instead of taking of it. But I live on broken wittles – and I sleep on the coals' – here the waiter burst into tears.

I was very much concerned for his misfortunes, and felt that any recognition short of ninepence would be mere brutality and hardness of heart. Therefore I gave him one of my three bright shillings, which he received with much humility and veneration, and spun up with his thumb, directly afterwards, to try the goodness of.

It was a little disconcerting to me to find, when I was being helped up behind the coach, that I was supposed to have eaten all the dinner without any assistance. I discovered this, from over-hearing the lady in the bow-window say to the guard, 'Take care of that child, George, or he'll burst!' and from observing that the women-servants who were about the place came out to look and giggle at me as a young phenomenon. My unfortunate friend the waiter, who had quite recovered his spirits, did not appear to be disturbed by this, but joined in the general admiration without being at all confused. If I had any doubt of him, I suppose this half-awakened it; but I am inclined to believe that with the simple confidence of a child, and the natural reliance of a child upon superior years (qualities I am very sorry any children should prematurely change for wordly wisdom), I had no serious mis-trust of him on the whole, even then.

I felt it rather hard, I must own, to be made, without deserving it, the subject of jokes between the coachman and guard as to the coach drawing heavy behind, on account of my sitting there, and as to the greater expediency of my travelling by waggon. The story of my supposed appetite getting wind among the outside passengers, they were merry upon it likewise; and asked me whether I was going to be paid for, at school, as two brothers or three, and whether I was contracted for, or went upon the regular terms; with other pleasant questions. But the worst of it was, that I knew I should be ashamed to eat anything when an opportunity offered, and that, after a rather light dinner, I should remain hungry all night – for I had left my cakes behind, at the hotel, in my hurry. My apprehensions were realised. When we stopped for supper I couldn't muster courage to take any, though I should have liked it very much, but sat by the fire and said I didn't want anything. This did not save me from more jokes, either; for a husky-voiced gentleman with a rough face, who had been eating out of a sandwich-box nearly all the way, except when he had been drinking out of a bottle, said I was like a boa-constrictor, who took enough at one meal to last him a long time; after which he actually brought a rash out upon himself with boiled beef.

We had started from Yarmouth at three o'clock in the afternoon, and we were due in London about eight next morning. It was midsummer weather, and the evening was very pleasant. When we passed through a village, I pictured to myself what the insides of the houses were like, and what the inhabitants were about; and when boys came running after us, and got up behind and swung there for a little way, I wondered whether their fathers were alive, and whether they were happy at home. I had plenty to think of, therefore, besides my mind running continually on the kind of place I was going to – which was an awful speculation. Sometimes, I remember, I resigned myself to thoughts of home and Peggotty; and to endeavour, in a confused blind way, to recall how I had felt, and what sort of boy I used to be, before I bit Mr Murdstone: which I couldn't satisfy myself about by any means, I seemed to have bitten him in such a remote antiquity.

The night was not so pleasant as the evening, for it got chilly; and being put between two gentlemen (the rough-faced one and another) to prevent my tumbling off the coach, I was nearly smothered by their falling asleep, and completely blocking me up. They squeezed me so hard sometimes, that I could not help crying out, 'Oh, if you please!' which they didn't like at all, because it woke them. Opposite me was an elderly lady in a great fur cloak, who looked in the dark more like a haystack than a lady, she was wrapped up to such a degree. This lady had a basket with her, and she hadn't known what to do with it for a long time, until she found that, on account of my legs being so short, it could go underneath me. It cramped and hurt me so, that it made me perfectly miserable; but if I moved in the least, and made a glass that was in the basket rattle against something else (as it was sure to do), she gave me the cruellest poke with her foot, and said, 'Come, don't *you* fidget. *Your* bones are young enough, *I'm* sure!'

At last the sun rose, and then my companions seemed to sleep easier. The difficulties under which they had laboured all night, and which had found utterance in the most terrific gasps and snorts, are not to be conceived. As the sun got higher, their sleep became lighter, and so they gradually one by one awoke. I recollect being very much surprised by the feint everybody made, then, of not having been to sleep at all, and by the uncommon indignation with which everyone repelled the charge. I labour under the same kind of astonishment to this day, having invariably observed that of all human weaknesses, the one to which our common nature is the least disposed to confess (I cannot imagine why) is the weakness of having gone to sleep in a coach.

What an amazing place London was to me when I saw it in the distance, and how I believed all the adventures of all my favourite heroes to be constantly enacting and re-enacting there, and how I vaguely made it out in my own mind to be fuller of wonders and wickedness than all the cities of the earth, I need not stop here to relate. We approached it by degrees, and got, in due time, to the inn in the Whitechapel district for which we were bound. I forget whether it was the Blue Bull, or the Blue Boar; but I know it was the Blue Something, and that its likeness was painted up on the back of the coach.

The guard's eye lighted on me as he was getting down, and he said at the booking-office door –

'Is there anybody here for a yoongster booked in the name of Murdstone, from Bloonderstone, Sooffolk, to be left till called for?'

Nobody answered.

'Try Copperfield, if you please, Sir,' said I, looking helplessly down.

'Is there anybody here for a yoongster, booked in the name of Murdstone, from Bloonderstone, Sooffolk, but owning to the name of Copperfield, to be left till called for?' said the guard. 'Come! *Is* there anybody?'

No. There was nobody. I looked anxiously around; but the inquiry made no impression on any of the bystanders, if I except a man in gaiters, with one eye, who suggested that they had better put a brass collar round my neck, and tie me up in the stable.

A ladder was brought, and I got down after the lady who was like a haystack: not daring to stir until her basket was removed. The coach was clear of passengers by that time, the luggage was very soon cleared out, the horses had been taken out before the luggage, and now the coach itself was wheeled and backed off by some hostlers, out of the way. Still, nobody appeared to claim the dusty youngster from Blunderstone, Suffolk.

More solitary than Robinson Crusoe, who had nobody to look at him and see that he was solitary, I went into the booking-office, and, by invitation of the clerk on duty, passed behind the counter, and sat down on the scale at which they weighed the luggage. Here, as I sat looking at the parcels, packages, and books, and inhaling the smell of stables (ever since associated with that morning), a procession of most tremendous considerations began to march through my mind. Supposing nobody should ever fetch me, how long would they consent to keep me there? Would they keep me long enough to spend seven shillings? Should I sleep at night in one of those wooden bins, with the other luggage, and wash myself at the pump in the yard in the morning; or should I be turned out every night, and expected to come again to be left till called for, when the office opened next day? Supposing there was no mistake in the case, and Mrs Murdstone had devised this plan to get rid of me, what should I do? If they allowed me to remain there until my seven shillings were spent, I couldn't hope to remain there when I began to starve. That would obviously be inconvenient and unpleasant to the customers, besides entailing on the Blue Whatever-it-was the risk of funeral expenses. If I started off at once, and tried to walk back home, how could I ever find my way, how could I ever hope to walk so far, how could I make sure of any one but Peggotty, even if I got back? If I found out the nearest proper authorities, and offered myself to go for a soldier or a sailor, I was such a little fellow that it was most likely they wouldn't take me in. These thoughts, and a hundred other such thoughts, turned me burning hot, and made me giddy with apprehension and dismay. I was in the height of my fever when a man entered and whispered to the clerk, who presently slanted me off the scale, and pushed me over to him, as if I were weighed, bought, delivered, and paid for.

As I went out of the office hand in hand with this new acquaintance, I stole a look at him. He was a gaunt, sallow young man, with hollow cheeks, and a chin almost as black as Mr Murdstone's; but there the likeness ended, for his whiskers were shaved off, and his hair, instead of being glossy, was rusty and dry. He was dressed in a suit of black clothes which were rather rusty and dry too, and rather short in the sleeves and legs; and he had a white neck-kerchief on, that was not over-clean. I did not, and do not,

suppose that this neck-kerchief was all the linen he wore, but it
was all he showed or gave any hint of.

'You're the new boy?' he said.

'Yes, Sir,' I said.

I supposed I was. I didn't know.

'I'm one of the masters at Salem House,' he said.

Charles Dickens (1812–1820), *David Copperfield*

CLIMBING-BOYS

Henry Mayhew wrote volumes telling of his research into the lives of the outcasts, the poor, and the unfortunate who had been driven to crime, in London. Here he is illustrating his account of the chimney-sweeping trade by an interview with an ex-sweeper.

'Yes, I was a climbing-boy, and sarved a rigler printiceship for seven years. I was out on my printiceship when I was fourteen. Father was a silk-weaver, and did all he knew to keep me from being a sweep, but I would be a sweep, and nothink else.' (This is not so very uncommon a predilection, strange as it may seem.) 'So father, when he saw it was no use, got me bound printice. Father's alive now, and near 90 years of age. I don't know why I wished to be a sweep, 'cept it was this – there was sweeps always lived about here, and I used to see the boys with lots of money a tossin' and gamblin', and wished to have money too. You see they got money where they swept the chimneys; they used to get 2d. or 3d. for theirselves in a day, and sometimes 6d. from the people of the house, and that's the way they always had plenty of money. I niver thought anythink of the climbing; it wasn't so bad at all as some people would make you believe. There are two or three ways of climbing. In wide flues you climb with your elbows and your legs spread out, your feet pressing against the sides of the flue; but in narrow flues, such as nine-inch ones, you must slant it; you must have your sides in the angles, it's wider there, and go up just that way.' (Here he threw himself into position – placing one arm close to his side, with the palm of the hand turned outwards, as if pressing the side of the flue, and extending the other arm high above his head, the hand apparently pressing in the same manner.) 'There,' he continued, 'that's slantin'. You just put yourself in that way, and see how small you make yourself. I niver got to say stuck myself, but a many of them did; yes, and were taken out dead. They were smothered for want of air, and the fright, and a stayin' so long in the flue; you see the waist-

147

band of their trousers sometimes got turned down in the climbing, and in narrow flues, when not able to get it up, then they
stuck. I had a boy once – we were called to sweep a chimney
down at Poplar. When we went in he looked up the flues, "Well,
what is it like?" I said. "Very narrow," says he, "don't think I
can get up there;" so after some time we gets on top of the house,
and takes off the chimney-pot, and has a look down – it was
wider a' top, and I thought as how he could go down. "You had
better buff it, Jim," says I. I suppose you know what that means;
but Jim wouldn't do it, and kept his trousers on. So down he goes,
and gets on very well till he comes to the shoulder of the flue, and
then he couldn't stir. He shouts down. "I'm stuck." I shouts up
and tells him what to do. "Can't move," says he, "I'm stuck hard
and fast." Well, the people of the house got fretted like, but I says
to them, "Now my boy's stuck, but for Heaven's sake don't make
a word of noise; don't say a word, good or bad, and I'll see what
I can do." So I locks the door, and buffs it, and forces myself up
till I could reach him with my hand, and as soon as he got his
foot on my hand he begins to prize himself up, and gets loosened,
and comes out at the top again. I was stuck myself, but I was
stronger nor he, and I manages to get out again. Now I'll be
bound to say if there was another master there as would kick up
a row and a-worrited, that ere boy 'ud a niver come out o' that
ere flue alive. There was a many o' them lost their lives in that
way. Most all the printices used to come from the "House"
(workhouse). There was nobody to care for them, and some
masters used them very bad. I was out of my time at fourteen,
and began to get too stout to go up the flues; so after knockin'
about a year or so, as I could do nothink else, I goes to sea on
board a man-o'-war, and was away four year. Many of the boys,
when they got too big and useless, used to go to sea in them days –
they couldn't do nothink else. Yes, many of them went for
sodgers; and I know some who went for gipsies, and others who
went for play-actors, and a many who got on to be swellmobsmen,
and thieves, and housebreakers, and the like o' that ere. There
ain't nothink o' that sort a-goin' on now since the Ack of Parlia-
ment. When I got back from sea father asked me to larn his
business; so I takes to the silk-weaving and larned it, and then
married a weaveress, and worked with father for a long time.
Father was very well off – well off and comfortable for a poor

man – but trade was good then. But it got bad afterwards, and none on us was able to live at it; so I takes to the chimney-sweeping again. A man might manage to live somehow at the sweeping, but the weaving was o' no use. It was the furrin silks as beat us all up, that's the whole truth. Yet they tells us as how they was a-doin' the country good; but they may tell that to the marines – the sailors won't believe it – not a word on it. I've stuck to the sweeping ever since, and sometimes done very fair at it; but since the Ack there's so many leeks come to it that I don't know how they live – they must be eatin' one another up.

'Well, since you ask then, I can tell you that our people don't care much about law; they don't understand anythink about politics much; they don't mind things o' that ere kind. They only minds to get drunk when they can. Some on them fellows as you seed in there niver cleans their selves from one year's end to the other. They'll kick up a row soon enough, with Chartists or any-body else. I thinks them Chartists are a weak-minded set; they was too much a frightened at nothink, – a hundred o' them would run away from one blue-coat, and that wasn't like men. I was often at Chartist meetings, and if they'd only do all they said there was a plenty to stick to them, for there's a somethink wants to be done very bad, for everythink is a-gettin' worser and worser every day. I used to do a good trade, but now I don't yarn a shilling a day all through the year. I may walk at this time three or four miles and not get a chimney to sweep, and then get only a sixpence or threepence, and sometimes nothink. It's a starvin', that's what it is; there's so much "querying" a-goin' on. Query-ing? that's what we calls under-working. If they'd all fix a riglar price we might do very well still. I'm 50 years of age or thereabouts.'

Some years back the sweepers' houses were often indicated by an elaborate sign, highly coloured. A sweeper, accompanied by a 'chummy' (once a common name for the climbing-boy, being a corruption of chimney), was depicted on his way to a red brick house, from the chimneys of which bright yellow flames were streaming. Below was the detail of the things undertaken by the sweep, such as the extinction of fires in chimneys, the cleaning of smoke-jacks, etc., etc. A few of these signs, greatly faded, may be seen still. A sweeper, who is settled in what is accounted a 'genteel neighbourhood,' has now another way of making his calling known. He leaves a card whenever he hears of a new comer, a tape being attached, so that it can be hung up in the kitchen, and thus the servants are always in possession of his address. The following is a customary style:

'Chimneys swept by the improved machine, much patronized by the Humane Society.

'W. H., Chimney Sweeper and Nightman, 1 – Mews, in returning thanks to the inhabitants of the surrounding neighbourhood for the patronage he has hitherto received, begs to inform them that he sweeps all kinds of chimneys and flues in the best manner.

'W. H., attending to the business himself, cleans smoke-jacks, cures smoky coppers, and extinguishes chimneys when on fire, with the greatest care and safety; and, by giving the strictest personal attendance to business, performs what he undertakes with cleanliness and punctuality, whereby he hopes to ensure a continuance of their favours and recommendations.

'Clean cloths for upper apartments. Soot-doors to any size fixed. Observe the address, 1 – Mews, near –'

At the top of this card is an engraving of the machine; at the foot a rude sketch of a nightman's cart, with men at work. All the cards I saw reiterated the address, so that no mistake might lead the customer to a rival tradesman.

Henry Mayhew (1812–1887),
London Labour and the Labouring Poor

THE FOOTBALL MATCH

Tom Brown's Schooldays, *written about a hundred and twenty years ago, gives us a picture of life at one of the boarding-schools that have come to be known as public schools.*

A goal in the first hour – such a thing hasn't been done in the School-house match this five years.

'Over!' is the cry: the two sides change goals, and the School-house goal-keeper come threading their way across through the masses of the School; the most openly triumphant of them, amongst whom is Tom, a School-house boy of two hours' standing, getting their ears boxed in the transit. Tom indeed is excited beyond measure, and it is all the sixth-form boy, kindest and safest of goal-keepers, has been able to do to keep him from rushing out whenever the ball has been near their goal. So he holds him by his side, and instructs him in the science of touching.

At this moment Griffith, the itinerant vendor of oranges from Hill Morton, enters the close with his heavy baskets; there is a rush of small boys upon the little pale-faced man, the two sides mingling together subdued by the great Goddess Thirst, like the English and French by the streams in the pyrenees. The leaders are past oranges and apples, but some of them visit their coats, and apply innocent-looking ginger-beer bottles to their mouths. It is no ginger-beer, though, I fear, and will do you no good. One short mad rush, and then a stitch in the side, and no more honest play; that's what comes of those bottles.

But now Griffith's baskets are empty, the ball is placed again midway, and the School are going to kick off. Their leaders have sent their lumber into goal, and rated the rest soundly, and one hundred and twenty picked players-up are there, bent on retrieving the game. They are to keep the ball in front of the School-house goal, and then to drive it in by sheer strength and weight. They mean heavy play and no mistake, and so old Brooke sees; and places Crab Jones in quarters just before the goal, with four or five picked players, who are to keep the ball away to the sides,

151

where a try at goal, if obtained, will be less dangerous than in
front. He himself, and Warner and Hedge, who have saved themselves till now, will lead the chargers.

'Are you ready?' 'Yes.' And away comes the ball kicked high
in the air, to give the School time to rush on and catch it as it
falls. And here they are amongst us. Meet them like Englishmen,
you School-house boys, and charge them home. Now is the time
so show what mettle is in you – and there shall be a warm seat by
the hall fire, and honour, and lots of bottled-beer tonight, for him
who does his duty in the next half-hour. And they are well met.
Again and again the cloud of their players-up gathers before our
goal, and comes threatening on, and Warner or Hedge, with young
Brooke and the relics of the bull-dogs, break through and carry
the ball back; and old Brooke ranges the field like Job's war-
horse, the thickest scrummage parts asunder before his rush, like
the waves before a clipper's bows; his cheery voice rings over the
field, and his eye is everywhere. And if these miss the ball, and
it rolls dangerously in front of our goal, Crab Jones and his men
have seized it and sent it away towards the sides with the unerring
drop-kick. This is worth living for; the whole sum of school-boy
existence gathered up into one straining, struggling half-hour, a
half-hour worth a year of common life. The quarter to five has
struck, and the play slackens for a minute before a goal; but there
is Crew, the artful dodger, driving the ball in behind our goal, on
the island side, where our quarters are weakest. Is there no one
to meet him? Yes! look at little East! the ball is just at equal
distances between the two, and they rush together, the young man
of seventeen and the boy of twelve, and kick it at the same
moment. Crew passes on without a stagger; East is hurled forward by the shock, and plunges on his shoulder, as if he would
bury himself in the ground; but the ball rises straight into the
air, and falls behind Crew's back, while the bravos of the School-
house attest the pluckiest charge of all that hard-fought day.
Warner picks up East lame and half stunned, and he hobbles back
into goal, conscious of having played the man.

And now the last minutes are come, and the School gather for
their last rush, every boy of the hundred and twenty who has a
run left in him. Reckless of the defence of their own goal, on they
come across the level big-side ground, the ball well down amongst
them, straight for our goal, like the column of the old guard up

the slope at Waterloo. All former charges have been child's play to this. Warner and Hedge have met them, but still on they come. The bull-dogs rush in for the last time; they are hurled over or carried back, striving hand, foot, and eyelids. Old Brooke comes sweeping round the skirts of the play, and turning short round, picks out the very heart of the scrummage, and plunges in. It wavers for a moment – he has the ball! No, it has passed him, and his voice rings out clear over the advancing tide, 'Look out in goal.' Crab Jones catches it for a moment, but before he can kick the rush is upon him and passes over him; and he picks himself up behind them with his straw in his mouth, a little dirtier, but as cool as ever.

The ball rolls slowly in behind the School-house goal, not three yards in front of a dozen of the biggest School players-up.

There stand the School-house praepostor, safest of goal-keepers, and Tom Brown by his side, who has learned his trade by this time. Now is your time, Tom. The blood of all the Browns is up, and the two rush in together, and throw themselves on the ball, under the very feet of the advancing column; the praepostor on his hands and knees arching his back, and Tom all along on his face. Over them topple the leaders of the rush, shooting over the back of the praepostor, but falling flat on Tom, and knocking all the wind out of his small carcase. 'Our ball,' says the prae-postor, rising with his prize; 'but get up there, there's a little fellow under you.' They are hauled up and roll off him, and Tom is discovered a motionless body.

Old Brooke picks him up. 'Stand back, give him air,' he says; and then feeling his limbs, adds, 'No bones broken. How do you feel, young 'un?'

'Hah-hah,' gasps Tom as his wind comes back, 'pretty well, thank you – all right.'

'Who is it he says?' says Brooke.

'Oh, it's Brown, he's a new boy; I know him,' says East, com-ing up.

'Well, he's a plucky youngster, and will make a player,' says Brooke.

And five o'clock strikes. 'No side' is called, and the first day of the School-house match is over.

Thomas Hughes (1822–1896), *Tom Brown's Schooldays*

THE RAFT

Huck Finn is helping his Negro friend Jim to escape to a part of America where he will be a slave no longer.

I went up the bank about fifty yards, and then I doubled on my tracks and slipped back to where my canoe was, a good piece below the house. I jumped in and was off in a hurry. I went up-stream far enough to make the head of the island, and then started across. I took off the sun-bonnet, for I didn't want no blinders on, then. When I was about the middle, I hear the clock begin to strike; so I stops and listens; the sound come faint over the water, but clear – eleven. When I struck the head of the island I never waited to blow, though I was most winded, but I shoved right into the timber where my old camp used to be, and started a good fire there on a high-and-dry spot.

Then I jumped in the canoe and dug out for our place a mile and a half below, as hard as I could go. I landed, and slopped through the timber and up the ridge and into the cavern. There Jim laid, sound asleep on the ground. I roused him out and says:

'Git up and hump yourself, Jim! There ain't a minute to lose. They're after us!'

Jim never asked no questions, he never said a word; but the way he worked for the next half an hour showed about how he was scared. By that time everything we had in the world was on our raft and she was ready to be shoved out from the willow cove where she was hid. We put out the camp-fire at the cavern the first thing, and didn't show a candle outside after that.

I took the canoe out from shore a little piece and took a look, but if there was a boat around I couldn't see it, for stars and shadows ain't good to see by. Then we got out the raft and slipped along down in the shade, past the foot of the island, dead still, never saying a word.

It must a been close on to one o'clock when we got below the island at last, and the raft did seem to go mighty slow. If a boat

was to come along, we was going to take to the canoe and break
for the Illinois shore; and it was well a boat didn't come, for we
hadn't ever thought to put the gun into the canoe, or a fishing-line
or anything to eat. We was in ruther too much of a sweat to think
of so many things. It warn't good judgment to put everything on
the raft.

If the men went to the island, I just expect they found the
camp-fire I built, and watched it all night for Jim to come. Any-
ways, they stayed away from us, and if my building the fire never
fooled them it warn't no fault of mine. I played it as low-down
on them as I could.

When the first streak of day begun to show, we tied up to a
tow-head in a big bend on the Illinois side, and hacked off
cotton-wood branches with the hatchet and covered up the raft
with them so she looked like there had been a cave-in in the bank
there. A tow-head is a sand-bar that has cotton-woods on it as
thick as harrow-teeth.

We had mountains on the Missouri shore and heavy timber on
the Illinois side, and the channel was down the Missouri shore at
that place, so we warn't afraid of anybody running across us. We
laid there all day and watched the rafts and steamboats spin down
the Missouri shore, and up-bound steamboats fight the big river
in the middle. I told Jim all about the time I had jabbering with
that woman; and Jim said she was a smart one, and if she was to
start after us herself she wouldn't set down and watch a camp-
fire – no, sir, she'd fetch a dog. Well, then, I said, why couldn't
she tell her husband to fetch a dog? Jim said he bet she did think
of it by the time the men was ready to start, and he believed they
must a gone up-town to get a dog, and so they lost all that time,
or else we wouldn't be here on a tow-head sixteen or seventeen
mile below the village – no, indeedy, we would be in that same
old town again. So I said I didn't care what was the reason they
didn't get us, as long as they didn't.

When it was beginning to come on dark, we poked our heads
out of the cotton-wood thicket and looked up, and down, and
across; nothing in sight; so Jim took up some of the top planks
of the raft and built a snug wigwam to get under in blazing
weather and rainy, and to keep the things dry. Jim made a floor
for the wigwam, and raised it a foot or more above the level of
the raft, so now the blankets and all the traps was out of the

reach of steamboat waves. Right in the middle of the wigwam we made a layer of dirt about five or six inches deep with a frame around it for to hold it to its place; this was to build a fire on in sloppy weather or chilly; the wigwam would keep it from being seen. We made an extra steering oar, too, because one of the others might get broke, on a snag or something. We fixed up a short forked stick to hang the old lantern on; because we must always light the lantern whenever we see a steamboat coming down-stream, to keep from getting run over; but we wouldn't have to light it for up-stream boats unless we see we was in what they call a 'crossing'; for the river was pretty high yet, very low banks being still a little under-water; so up-bound boats didn't always run the channel, but hunted easy water.

This second night we run between seven and eight hours, with a current that was making over four mile an hour. We catched fish, and talked, and we took a swim now and then to keep off sleepiness. It was kind of solemn, drifting down the big still river, laying on our backs looking up at the stars, and we didn't ever feel like talking loud, and it warn't often that we laughed, only a little kind of a low chuckle. We had mighty good weather, as a general thing, and nothing ever happened to us at all, that night, nor the next, nor the next.

Every night we passed towns, some of them away up on black hill-sides, nothing but just a shiny bed of lights, not a house could you see. The fifth night we passed St. Louis, and it was like the whole world lit up. In St. Petersburg they used to say there was twenty or thirty thousand people in St. Louis, but I never believed it till I see that wonderful spread of lights at two o'clock that still night. There warn't a sound there; everybody was asleep.

Every night, now, I used to slip ashore, towards ten o'clock, at some little village, and buy ten or fifteen cents' worth of meal or bacon or other stuff to eat; and sometimes I lifted a chicken that warn't roosting comfortable, and took him along. Pap always said, take a chicken when you get a chance, because if you don't want him yourself you can easy find somebody that does, and a good deed ain't ever forgot. I never see pap when he didn't want the chicken himself, but that is what he used to say, anyway.

Mornings, before daylight, I slipped into corn-fields and borrowed a watermelon, or a mushmelon, or a punkin, or some new corn, or things of that kind. Pap always said it warn't no harm to borrow things, if you was meaning to pay them back, some-time; but the widow said it warn't anything but a soft name for stealing, and no decent body would do it. Jim said he reckoned the widow was partly right and pap was partly right; so the best way would be for us to pick out two or three things from the list and say we wouldn't borrow them any more – then he reckoned it wouldn't be no harm to borrow the others. So we talked it over all one night, drifting along down the river, trying to make up our minds whether to drop the watermelons, or the cantelopes, or the mushmelons, or what. But towards daylight we got it all settled satisfactorily, and concluded to drop crab-apples and p'simmons. We warn't feeling just right before that, but it was all comfortable now. I was glad the way it came out, too, because crab-apples ain't ever good, and the p'simmons wouldn't be ripe for two or three months yet.

Mark Twain (1835–1910), *Huckleberry Finn*

TOM TULLIVER

Mr and Mrs Tulliver live in a comfortable house next their mill.
They have a daughter, Maggie, who is thoughtful, clever and quiet,
and a son, Tom, who is fond of outdoor pursuits, but not of books
and learning. Mr Tulliver wants Tom educated, so he sends him
away to a tutor, Mr Stelling.

In his secret heart he yearned to have Maggie with him, and was
almost ready to dote on her exasperating acts of forgetfulness;
though, when he was at home, he always represented it as a great
favour on his part to let Maggie trot by his side on his pleasure
excursions.

And before this dreary half-year was ended, Maggie actually
came. Mrs Stelling had given a general invitation for the little
girl to come and stay with her brother: so when Mr Tulliver
drove over to King's Lorton late in October, Maggie came too,
with the sense that she was taking a great journey, and beginning
to see the world. It was Mr Tulliver's first visit to see Tom, for
the lad must learn not to think too much about home.

'Well, my lad,' he said to Tom, when Mr Stelling had left the
room to announce the arrival to his wife, and Maggie had begun
to kiss Tom freely, 'you look rarely! School agrees with you.'

Tom wished he had looked rather ill.

'I don't think I *am* well, father,' said Tom; 'I wish you'd ask
Mr Stelling not to let me do Euclid – it brings on the toothache,
I think.'

(The toothache was the only malady to which Tom had ever
been subject.)

'Euclid, my lad – why, what's that?' said Mr Tulliver.

'Oh, I don't know: its definitions, and axioms, and triangles,
and things. It's a book I've got to learn in – there's no sense in it.'

'Go, go!' said Mr Tulliver reprovingly, 'you mustn't say so.
You must learn what your master tells you. He knows what it's
right for you to learn.'

'*I'll* help you now, Tom,' said Maggie, with a little air of patronising consolation. 'I'm come to stay ever so long, if Mrs Stelling asks me. I've brought my box and my pinafores, haven't I, father?'

'*You* help me, you silly little thing!' said Tom, in such high spirits at this announcement that he quite enjoyed the idea of confounding Maggie by showing her a page of Euclid. 'I should like to see you doing one of *my* lessons! Why, I learn Latin too! Girls never learn such things. They're too silly.'

'I know what Latin is very well,' said Maggie confidently. 'Latin's a language. There are Latin words in the Dictionary. There's bonus, a gift.'

'Now, you're just wrong there, Miss Maggie!' said Tom, secretly astonished. 'You think you're very wise! But "bonus" means "good," as it happens – bonus, bona, bonum.'

'Well, that's no reason why it shouldn't mean "gift," ' said Maggie stoutly. 'It may mean several things – almost every word does. There's "lawn" – it means the grass-plot, as well as the stuff pocket-handkerchiefs are made of.'

'Well done, little 'un,' said Mr Tulliver, laughing, while Tom felt rather disgusted with Maggie's knowingness, though beyond measure cheerful at the thought that she was going to stay with him. Her conceit would soon be overawed by the actual inspection of his books.

Mrs Stelling, in her pressing invitation, did not mention a longer time than a week for Maggie's stay; but Mr Stelling, who took her between his knees, and asked her where she stole her dark eyes from, insisted that she must stay a fortnight. Maggie thought Mr Stelling was a charming man, and Mr Tulliver was quite proud to leave his little wench where she would have an opportunity of showing her cleverness to appreciating strangers. So it was agreed that she should not be fetched home till the end of the fortnight.

'Now, then, come with me into the study, Maggie,' said Tom, as their father drove away. 'What do you shake and toss your head now for, you silly?' he continued; for though her hair was now under a dispensation, and was brushed smoothly behind her ears, she seemed still in imagination to be tossing it out of her eyes. 'It makes you look as if you were crazy.'

'Oh, I can't help it,' said Maggie impatiently. 'Don't tease me,

Tom. Oh, what books!' she exclaimed, as she saw the bookcases
in the study. 'How I should like to have as many books as that!'

'Why, you couldn't read one of 'em,' said Tom triumphantly.
'They're all Latin.'

'No, they aren't,' said Maggie. 'I can read the back of this . . .
"History of the Decline and Fall of the Roman Empire." '

'Well, what does that mean? *You* don't know,' said Tom,
wagging his head.

'But I could soon find out,' said Maggie scornfully.

'Why, how?'

'I should look inside, and see what it was about.'

'You'd better not, Miss Maggie,' said Tom, seeing her hand
on the volume. 'Mr Stelling lets nobody touch his books without
leave, and *I* shall catch it, if you take it out.'

'Oh, very well! Let me see all *your* books, then,' said Maggie,
turning to throw her arms round Tom's neck, and rub his cheek
with her small round nose.

Tom, in the gladness of his heart at having dear old Maggie
to dispute with and crow over again, seized her round the waist,
and began to jump with her round the large library table. Away
they jumped with more and more vigour, till Maggie's hair flew
from behind her ears, and twirled about like an animated mop.
But the revolutions round the table became more and more
irregular in their sweep, till at last reaching Mr Stelling's reading-
stand, they sent it thundering down with its heavy lexicons to the
floor. Happily it was the ground-floor, and the study was a one-
storied wing to the house, so that the downfall made no alarming
resonance, though Tom stood dizzy and aghast for a few minutes,
dreading the appearance of Mr or Mrs Stelling.

'Oh, I say, Maggie,' said Tom at last, lifting up the stand, 'we
must keep quiet here, you know. If we break anything, Mrs
Stelling'll make us cry peccavi.'

'What's that?' said Maggie.

'Oh, it's the Latin for a good scolding,' said Tom, not without
some pride in his knowledge.

'Is she a cross woman?' said Maggie.

'I believe you!' said Tom, with an emphatic nod.

'I think all women are crosser than men,' said Maggie. 'Aunt
Glegg's a great deal crosser than Uncle Glegg, and mother scolds
me more than father does.'

'Well, *you'll* be a woman some day,' said Tom, 'so *you* needn't talk.'

'But I shall be a *clever* woman,' said Maggie, with a toss.

'Oh, I dare say, and a nasty conceited thing. Everybody'll hate you.'

'But you oughtn't to hate me, Tom: it'll be very wicked of you, for I shall be your sister.'

'Yes, but if you're a nasty disagreeable thing, I *shall* hate you.'

'Oh but, Tom, you won't! I shan't be disagreeable. I shall be very good to you – and I shall be good to everybody. You won't hate me really, will you, Tom?'

'Oh, bother! never mind! Come it's time for me to learn my lessons. See here! what I've got to do,' said Tom, drawing Maggie towards him and showing her his theorem, while she pushed her hair behind her ears, and prepared herself to prove her capability of helping him in Euclid. She began to read with full confidence in her own powers, but presently, becoming quite bewildered, her face flushed with irritation. It was unavoidable – she must confess her incompetency, and she was not fond of humiliation.

'It's nonsense!' she said, 'and very ugly stuff – nobody need want to make it out.'

'Ah, there now, Miss Maggie!' said Tom, drawing the book away, and wagging his head at her; 'you see you're not so clever as you thought you were.'

'Oh,' said Maggie, pouting, 'I dare say I could make it out if I'd learned what goes before, as you have.'

'But that's what you just couldn't, Miss Wisdom,' said Tom. 'For it's all the harder when you know what goes before: for then you've got to say what definition 3 is, and what axiom V. is. But get along with you now: I must go on with this. Here's the Latin Grammar. See what you can make of that.'

Maggie found the Latin Grammar quite soothing after her mathematical mortification; for she delighted in new words, and quickly found that there was an English Key at the end, which would make her very wise about Latin, at slight expense. She presently made up her mind to skip the rules in the Syntax – the examples became so absorbing. These mysterious sentences, snatched from an unknown context – like strange horns of beasts and leaves of unknown plants, brought from some far-off region –

gave boundless scope to her imagination, and were all the more fascinating because they were in a peculiar tongue of their own, which she could learn to interpret. It was really very interesting – the Latin Grammar that Tom had said no girls could learn; and she was proud because she found it interesting. The most fragmentary examples were her favourites. *Mors omnibus est communis* would have been jejune, only she liked to know the Latin; but the fortunate gentleman whom every one congratulated because he had a son 'endowed with *such* a disposition' afforded her a great deal of pleasant conjecture, and she was quite lost in the 'thick grove penetrable by no star,' when Tom called out –

'Now, then, Magsie, give us the Grammar!'

'Oh, Tom, it's such a pretty book!' she said, as she jumped out of the large arm-chair to give it him; 'it's much prettier than the Dictionary. I could learn Latin very soon. I don't think it's at all hard.'

'Oh, I know what you've been doing,' said Tom; 'You've been reading the English at the end. Any donkey can do that.'

Tom seized the book and opened it with a determined and business-like air, as much as to say that he had a lesson to learn which no donkeys would find themselves equal to. Maggie, rather piqued, turned to the bookcases to amuse herself with puzzling out the titles.

George Eliot (1819–1880), *The Mill on the Floss*

THE SWARMING OF THE BEES

Will comes home from school to find his father – Harry Price – and grandfather – Jack Price – ready to catch the swarming bees.

One day as he rode up the lane from school, he heard a strange high shouting, beyond the patch. He ran his bike along the hedge by the holly, and followed the shouting. Across the drying green, by the apple-trees, Harry and Jack Price were shouting and dancing, clapping their hands above their heads. Above them, twenty feet in the air and still rising, a swarm of bees moved in a gathering brown cloud. Will had seen many swarms, but the first thing he noticed, now, was the way his father and grandfather were dancing; the bees seemed only an excuse. And then Ellen arrived, carrying a zinc bath full of pans, and they all took the pans and began a furious drumming and clattering on them. The brown cloud rose steadily higher, above the apple trees. Still, the tanging continued, and the excited shouting. Then suddenly, 'they're going,' Ellen shouted, and at once the tanging was stopped and Harry was running away down the green, through the hedge by his garden, and into the field beyond. The cloud was against the sun, flying west to the mountains. 'And you, boy,' Jack Price shouted. Will ran back through the patch, and fetched his bike. The excitement was still racing in him, as he rode down the patch to the road. At the shop Harry was waiting, and took the bike. Will went on, across country. The swarm was far ahead of them now, but they had got its direction.

Will ran down the field, past Elwyn's cottage, to the plank bridge over the river. He made for the opening through the railway embankment. A goods train was passing on the down line, the engine labouring and sending out a great grey cloud of smoke. The fireman was shying knobs of coal at the scurrying rabbits along the embankment. Elwyn always said how much coal they got there, 'coal and rabbits from the same bank.' Stubby stalactites hung from the grey arch under the line. Beyond was a wide view of the rising ground to the mountain. He climbed on a stile and looked up into the sky. There was nothing, not even a bird. He looked back towards the patch and then at the trees to see the direction of the wind. But it was very slight, hardly more than a breath. After two more fields he reached the deep cutting of the old road. It was deserted and silent.

He called, but there was no answer. He walked north, listening. Then, round a bend, he saw his bike lying on its side in a bed of nettles, the back wheel still slowly spinning. There was a glat beyond the nettles, and a path to the mountain. He called again, and then ran up the path. A long narrow wood lay ahead, and as he passed through it, to the steep bracken rise, he heard Harry call. At the end of a narrow field, on the edge of a dingle, Harry stood looking up at the bees. They were settling on a branch about seven feet from the ground, the brown crawling beard slowly growing in size. As Will came up, Harry was laughing exultantly. The sweat had made little runnels of dirt down his cheeks, and his hair was wet and matted to his head. The leg of his trousers had been torn, and Will could see the dotted red line of the scratch underneath. But the luck of finding the bees was everything.

The bees settled slowly, and the branch looped gracefully with their weight.

'Watch them, but keep away!' Harry said. 'I'll go back for my kit.'

'If they go again shall I keep after them?'

'Just stay.'

It was forty minutes before Harry got back to the swarm. He came up the field, carrying the two-handled zinc bath at his chest. In the bath was a box, with his gauntlets and veil and blower.

'All quiet?'

'Aye, it's humming now, not buzzing.'

'Aye, they're settling.'

Harry took the bath and carried it down into the dingle. He set it upside down, immediately below the swarm. Then, setting the lid very carefully against the bath, he put the box beside it. He stuffed the cloth into the waistband of his trousers, then tucked his trouser ends inside his socks, and put on the veil, which was sewn to the brim of an old felt hat. He drew the bottom of the veil tightly around his neck, then crouched and took up the blower. He unscrewed the back and pulled out an edge of the rolled corrugated paper, and lit it with a match. He screwed up again, and stood testing the bellows. A thin trail of acrid blue smoke came from the long spout. Putting the blower under his arm, he pulled on his gauntlets, and looked round the dingle.

'Shall I come, Dad?'

'No, you keep right back.' The voice was muffled by the veil.

Harry walked carefully around the swarm, seeing how the branch lay in relation to the main bush. Then he touched the lid again and bent and picked up the open wooden box. He got up on to the bath, and slowly lifted the box past his chest, until it rested at one end of his shoulder. The bees were already disturbed; several were flying around his hands, and the noise had thinned and sharpened. He shifted his feet on the bath, and reached up past the swarm to grip the branch. He tested it with a very light pull, and checked again the position of the box. Scores of bees were now flying around, but he could not use the blower, which was in the hand holding the other end of the box. He hesitated and then suddenly pulled downwards on the branch, with his whole weight. At the same moment, with a heave of his shoulder, he thrust the box up around the swarm. There was an immediate violent buzzing, and a cloud of bees around his head. With his right hand he was now violently shaking the branch, getting the swarm free. He stepped down, one foot slipping from the bath as he staggered under the weight of the box. He let the box go down and grabbed for the lid, clapping it over the box. He pulled the cloth from his waistband and spread it quickly over the lid. He was surrounded now by a cloud of angry bees: so many, indeed, that there might almost be none in the box. He stood up and used his smoke blower, moving away. Slowly the bees circled away from him, and then went down to crawl over the box and the cloth. Puffing the thin smoke, Harry walked up the dingle, a strange figure in the veiled hat and the long gloves.

'Mind, keep away, till they've settled down.'

He stood picking bees from his clothes, throwing them lightly down towards the box, in which the angry buzzing continued.

Then he picked a stone and set it on the lid. Walking away, he smoked carefully all over his body, and then started taking off the gauntlets. Finally he took off the veiled hat, turned it upside-down and picked a bee from inside it.

'They'll take some carrying home, won't they?'

'You keep away. I'll manage them on the bike.'

'Shall I carry the other stuff?'

'No, you can't manage that. We'll leave the bath, get it to-morrow.'

'I can take the blower and the hat and so on.'

'Aye. In a few minutes.'

Harry squatted, and eased his shoulders. Down on the box, a hundred or more bees were crawling over the cloth. After a few minutes he put on the gloves and hat again, and, sliding back the lid a few inches, got most of the stragglers in. Then he crouched by the box, feeling under its edges with his fingers. Will saw him take the strain, and then lift suddenly.

'Go on, get away,' Harry shouted, coming straight up the dingle.

Will walked beside him, carrying the blower and sending out smoke at the bees that were still loose and following them. While he was enjoying this, he caught a glimpse of Harry's face, and stopped. He was walking awkwardly, with the box across his chest, but all the strain seemed to be in the face: the lips drawn back, baring the big teeth; the eyes narrowed; the forehead knotted and red.

'You'll have to rest them Dad. You won't get all the way down.'

Harry did not answer: he was watching the ground ahead of him, choosing his path. Will walked beside him, seeing the road come nearer. At last they reached the fence and Harry bent to put the heavy box on the grass.

'Get the bike. We shall be all right now.'

Will scrambled over the fence and wheeled the bike over the grass. Harry lifted the box to the fence, and climbed over, balancing it.

'Hold the bars.'

When the bike was firm, he lowered the box across the carrier. He pulled out a length of the hairy white string he always carried, and took two loops around the box and over the saddle.

'There's a couple of hundred pounds of honey, if I can keep them.'

He steadied the box while Will pushed, and they turned on the circle for home.

Raymond Williams (1921–   ), *Border Country*

THE ANTARCTIC EXPEDITION

In Bevis *Richard Jefferies describes his childhood as he would have liked it to be. Near the farm where he lived was a lake, in which he and his friends sailed and swam and fished. It had an island too, on which they built a hut where they lived secretly.*

The winter remained mild till early in January when the first green leaves had appeared on the woodbine. One evening Polly announced that it was going to freeze, for the cat as he sat on the hearthrug had put his paw over his ear. If he sat with his back to the fire, that was a sign of rain. If he put his paw over his ear that indicated frost.

It did freeze and hard. The wind being still, the New Sea was soon frozen over except in two places. There was a breathing-hole in Fir-Tree Gulf about fifty or sixty yards from the mouth of the Nile. The channel between New Formosa and Serendib did not 'catch', perhaps the current from Sweet River Falls was the cause, and though they could skate up within twenty yards, they could not land on the islands. Jack and Frances came to skate day after day; Bevis and Mark with Ted, Cecil, and the rest fought hockey battles for hours together.

One afternoon, being a little tired, Bevis sat on the ice, and presently lay down for a moment at full length, when looking along the ice – as he looked along his gun – he found he could see sticks or stones or anything that chanced to be on it a great distance off. Trying it again he could see the skates of some people very nearly half a mile distant, though his eyes were close to the surface, even if he placed the side of his head actually on the ice. The skates gleamed in the sun, and he could see them distinctly; sticks lying on the ice were not clearly seen so far as that, but a long way, so that the ice seemed perfectly level.

Suddenly there was a sound like the boom of a cannon and a crack shot across the broad water from shore to shore. The 'who-hoo-whoop' of the noise echoed back from the wood on the hill, and then they heard it again in the coombes and valleys, rolling along. As the ice was four or five inches thick it parted with a hollow roar: the crack sometimes forked, and a second running report followed the first. Sometimes the crack seemed to happen simultaneously all across the water. Occasionally they could hear it coming, and with a distinct interval of time before it reached them.

Up through these cracks or splits a little water oozed, and freezing on the surface formed barriers of rough ice from shore to shore, which jarred the skates as they passed over. These splits in no degree impaired the strength of the ice. Later on as they retired they opened the window and heard the boom again, weird and strange in the silence of the night.

One day a rabbit was started from a bunch of frozen rushes by the shore, and they chased it on the ice, overtaking it with ease. They could have knocked it down with hockey sticks, but forebore to do so. From these rush-bunches they now and then flushed dab-chicks or lesser grebes which, when there is open water, cannot be got to fly.

Till now the air had been still, but presently the wind blew from the south almost a gale; this was straight down the water, so keeping their skates together and spreading out their coats for sails they drove before the wind at a tremendous pace, flying past the trees and accumulating such velocity that their ankles ached from the vibration of the skates. Nor could they stop by any other means than describing a wide circle, and so gradually facing the wind. The thaw was a great disappointment.

The immense waves of ocean rise before the wind, and so the wind rushing over the ice no longer firm and rigid quickly broke up the surface, and there was a tremendous grinding and splintering, and chafing of the fragments. For the first few days these were carried down the New Sea, but presently the wind changed. The black north swooped on the earth and swept across the waters. Fields, trees, woods, hills, the very houses looked dark and hard, the water grey, the sky cold and dusky. The broken ice drifted before it and was all swept up to the other end of the New Sea and jammed between and about the islands. They could now get at the 'Pinta', and resolved to have a sail.

'An arctic expedition!'

'Antarctic – it is south'.

'All right'.

'Let us go to New Formosa'.

'So we will. But the ice is jammed there'.

'Cut through it'.

'Make an ice-bow'.

'Be quick'.

Up in the workshop they quickly nailed two short boards together like a V. This was lashed to the stem of the 'Pinta' to
protect her when they crashed into the ice. They took a reef in
the mainsail, for though the wind does not seem to travel any
swifter, yet in winter it somehow feels more hard and compact
and has a greater power on what it presses against. Just before
they cast loose, Frances appeared on the bank above; she had
called at the house, and hearing what they were about, hastened
up to join the expedition. So soon as she had got a comfortable
seat, well wrapped up in sealskin and muff, they pushed off,
and the 'Pinta' began to run before the wind. It was very strong,
much stronger than it had seemed ashore, pushing against the
sail as if it were a solid thing. The waves followed, and the grey
cold water lapped at the stern.

Beyond the battle-field as they entered the broadest and most
open part the black north roared and rushed at them, as if the
pressure of the sky descending forced a furious blast between it
and the surface. Angry and repellent waves hissed as their crests
blew off in cold foam and spray, stinging their cheeks. Ahead the
red sun was sinking over New Formosa, they raced towards the
disc, the sail straining as if it would split. As the boat drew near
they saw the ice jammed in the channel between the two islands.

It was thin and all in fragments; some under water, some piled
by the waves above the rest, some almost perpendicular, like
a sheet of glass standing upright and reflecting the red sunset.
Against the cliff the waves breaking threw fragments of ice
smashed into pieces; ice and spray rushed up the steep sand and
slid down again. But it was between the islands that the waves
wreaked with fury. The edge of the ice was torn into jagged bits
which dashed against each other, their white saw-like points
now appearing, now forced under by a large block.

Farther in the ice heaved as the waves rolled under: its surface
was formed of plates like a row of books fallen aside. As the ice
heaved these plates slid on each other, while others underneath

striving to rise to the surface struck and cracked them. Down
came the black north as a man might bring a sledge-hammer on
the anvil, the waves hissed, and turned darker, a white seagull
(which had come inland) rose to a higher level with easy strokes
of its wings.

Splinter – splanter! Crash! grind, roar; a noise like thousands
of gnashing teeth.

Bevis had his hand on the tiller; Mark his on the halyard of
the mainsail; neither spoke, it looked doubtful. The next instant
the 'Pinta' struck the ice midway between the islands, and the
impetus with which she came drove her six or seven feet clear
into the splintering fragments. They were jerked forwards, and
in an instant the following wave broke over the stern, and then
another, flooding the bottom of the boat. Mark had the mainsail
down, for it would have torn the mast out.

With a splintering, grinding, crashing, roaring, a horrible and
inexpressible noise of chaos – an orderless, rhythmless noise of
chaos – the mass gave way and swept slowly through the channel.
The impact of the boat acted like a battering ram and started the
jam. Fortunate it was for them that it did so, or the boat might
have been swamped by the following waves. Bevis got out a scull,
so did Mark, and their exertions kept her straight; had she
turned broadside it would have been awkward even as it was.
They swept through the channel, the ice at its edges barking
willow branches and planing the shore, large plates were forced
up high and dry.

'Hurrah!' shouted Mark.

'Hurrah!'

At the noise of their shouting thousands of starlings rose from
the osiers on Serendib with a loud rush of wings, blackening the
air like a cloud. They were soon through the channel, the ice
spread in the open water, and they worked the boat under shelter
of New Formosa, and landed.

'You are wet,' said Bevis as he helped Frances out.

'But it's jolly!' said Frances, laughing. 'Only think what a
fright he would have been in if he had known!'

Having made the boat safe – there was a lot of water in her –
they walked along the old path, now covered with dead leaves
damp from the thaw, to the stockade. The place was strewn with
small branches whirled from the trees by the gales, and in the

hut and further corner of the cave were heaps of brown oak leaves which had drifted in. Nothing else had changed: so well had they built it that the roof had neither broken down nor been destroyed by the winds.

During the frost a blackbird had roosted in a corner of the hut under the rafters, sparrows too had sought its shelter, and wrens and blue-tits had crept into the crevices of the eaves. Next they went up on the cliff, the sundial stood as they had left it, but the sun was now down.

From the height, where they could hardly stand against the wind, they saw a figure afar on the green hill by the sycamores, which they knew must be Big Jack waiting for them to return. Walking back to the 'Pinta' they passed under the now leafless teak tree marked and scored by the bullets they had fired at it.

Before embarking they baled out the water in the boat, and then inclined her, first one side and then the other, to see if she had sprung a leak, but she had not. The ice-bow was then hoisted on board, as it would no longer be required, and would impede their sailing. Frances stepped in, and Bevis and Mark settled themselves to row out of the channel. With such a wind it was impossible to tack in the narrow straight between the islands. They had to pull their very hardest to get through. So soon as they had got an offing the sculls were shipped, and the sails hoisted, but before they could get them to work they were blown back within thirty yards of the cliff. Then the sails drew, and they forged ahead.

It was the roughest voyage they had ever had. The wind was dead against them, and no matter on which tack every wave sent its spray, and sometimes the whole of its crest over the bows. The shock sometimes seemed to hold the 'Pinta' in mid-career, and her timbers trembled. Then she leaped forward and cut through, showering the spray aside. Frances laughed and sang, though the words were inaudible in the hiss and roar and the rush of the gale through the rigging, and the sharp, whip-like cracks of the fluttering pennant.

The velocity of their course carried them to and from the darkening waters in a few minutes, but the dusk fell quickly, and by the time they had reached Fir Tree Gulf, where they could get a still longer 'leg' or tack, the evening gloom had settled down. Big Jack stood on the shore, and beckoned them to come in:

they could easily have landed Frances under the lee of the hill, but she said she should go all the way now. So they tacked through the Mozambique, past Thessaly and the bluff, the waves getting less in size as they approached the northern shore, till they glided into the harbour. Jack had walked round and met them. He held out his hand, and Frances sprang ashore. 'How could you?' he said, in a tone of indignant relief. To him it had looked a terrible risk.

'Why it was splendid!' said Frances, and they went on together towards Longcot. Bevis and Mark stayed to furl sails, and leave the 'Pinta' ship-shape. By the time they had finished it was already dark: the night had come.

Richard Jefferies (1848–1887), *Bevis*

INJUSTICE

The novelist James Joyce was brought up at Catholic schools in Ireland, and describes his education in A Portrait of the Artist as a Young Man. *Though he gives himself the name of Stephen Dedalus in the book, it is really an autobiography. Here a senior master in priestly dress is going the rounds and speaks to Stephen:*

– You, boy, who are you?
Stephen's heart jumped suddenly.
– Dedalus, sir.
– Why are you not writing like the others?
– I ... my ...
He could not speak with fright.
– Why is he not writing, Father Arnall?
– He broke his glasses, said Father Arnall, and I exempted him from work.
– Broke? What is this I hear? What is this your name is? said the prefect of studies.
– Dedalus, sir.
– Out here, Dedalus. Lazy little schemer. I see schemer in your face. Where did you break your glasses?
Stephen stumbled into the middle of the class, blinded by fear and haste.
– Where did you break your glasses? repeated the prefect of studies.
– The cinderpath, sir.
– Hoho! The cinderpath! cried the prefect of studies. I know that trick.
Stephen lifted his eyes in wonder and saw for a moment Father Dolan's whitegrey not young face, his baldy whitegrey head with fluff at the sides of it, the steel rims of his spectacles and his nocoloured eyes looking through the glasses. Why did he say he knew that trick?
– Lazy idle little loafer! cried the prefect of studies. Broke my glasses! An old schoolboy trick! Out with your hand this moment!

Stephen closed his eyes and held out in the air his trembling hand with the palm upwards. He felt the prefect of studies touch it for a moment at the fingers to straighten it and then the swish of the sleeve of the soutane as the pandybat was lifted to strike. A hot burning stinging tingling blow like the loud crack of a broken stick made his trembling hand crumple together like a leaf in the fire: and at the sound and the pain scalding tears were driven into his eyes. His whole body was shaking with fright, his arm was shaking and his crumpled burning livid hand shook like a loose leaf in the air. A cry sprang to his lips, a prayer to be let off. But though the tears scalded his eyes and his limbs quivered with pain and fright he held back the hot tears and the cry that scalded his throat.

– Other hand! shouted the prefect of studies.

Stephen drew back his maimed and quivering right arm and held out his left hand. The soutane sleeve swished again as the pandybat was lifted and a loud crashing sound and a fierce maddening tingling burning pain made his hand shrink together with the palms and fingers in a livid quivering mass. The scalding water burst forth from his eyes and, burning with shame and agony and fear, he drew back his shaking arm in terror and burst out into a whine of pain. His body shook with a palsy of fright and in shame and rage he felt the scalding cry come from his throat and the scalding tears falling out of his eyes and down his flaming cheeks.

– Kneel down, cried the prefect of studies.

Stephen knelt down quickly pressing his beaten hands to his sides. To think of them beaten and swollen with pain all in a moment made him feel so sorry for them as if they were not his own but someone else's that he felt sorry for. And as he knelt, calming the last sobs in his throat and feeling the burning tingling pain pressed into his sides, he thought of the hands which he had held out in the air with the palms up and of the firm touch of the prefect of studies when he had steadied the shaking fingers and of the beaten swollen reddened mass of palm and fingers that shook helplessly in the air.

– Get at your work, all of you, cried the prefect of studies from the door. Father Dolan will be in every day to see if any boy any lazy idle little loafer wants flogging. Every day. Every day.

The door closed behind him.

The hushed class continued to copy out the themes. Father Arnall rose from his seat and went among them, helping the boys with gentle words and telling them the mistakes they had made. His voice was very gentle and soft. Then he returned to his seat and said to Fleming and Stephen:

– You may return to your places, you two.

Fleming and Stephen rose and, walking to their seats, sat down. Stephen, scarlet with shame, opened a book quickly with one weak hand and bent down upon it, his face close to the page.

It was unfair and cruel because the doctor had told him not to read without glasses and he had written home to his father that morning to send him a new pair. And Father Arnall had said that he need not study till the new glasses came. Then to be called a schemer before the class and to be pandied when he always got the card for first or second and was the leader of the Yorkists! How could the prefect of studies know that it was a trick? He felt the touch of the prefect's fingers as they had studied his hand and at first he had thought he was going to shake hands with him because the fingers were soft and firm: but then in an instant he had heard the swish of the soutane sleeve and the crash. It was cruel and unfair to make him kneel in the middle of the class then: and Father Arnall had told them both that they might return to their places without making any difference between them. He listened to Father Arnall's low and gentle voice as he corrected the themes. Perhaps he was sorry now and wanted to be decent. But it was unfair and cruel. The prefect of studies was a priest but that was cruel and unfair. And his white-grey face and the nocoloured eyes behind the steel rimmed spectacles were cruel looking because he had steadied the hand first with his firm soft fingers and that was to hit it better and louder.

– It's a stinking mean thing, that's what it is, said Fleming in the corridor as the classes were passing out in file to the refectory, to pandy a fellow for what is not his fault.

– You really broke your glasses by accident, didn't you? Nasty Roche asked.

Stephen felt his heart filled by Fleming's words and did not answer.

–Of course he did! said Fleming. I wouldn't stand it. I'd go up and tell the rector on him.

–Yes, said Cecil Thunder eagerly, and I saw him lift the pandy-
bat over his shoulder and he's not allowed to do that.
– Did they hurt you much? Nasty Roche asked.
– Very much, Stephen said.
– I wouldn't stand it, Fleming repeated, from Baldyhead or any
other Baldyhead. It's a stinking mean low trick, that's what it is.
I'd go straight up to the rector and tell him about it after dinner.
– Yes, do. Yes, do, said Cecil Thunder.
– Yes, do. Yes, go up and tell the rector on him, Dedalus, said
Nasty Roche, because he said that he'd come in tomorrow again
and pandy you.
– Yes, yes. Tell the rector, all said.

And there were some fellows out of second of grammar listening and one of them said:
– The senate and the Roman people declared that Dedalus had
been wrongly punished.

It was wrong; it was unfair and cruel; and, as he sat in the
refectory, he suffered time after time in memory the same
humiliation until he began to wonder whether it might not really
be that there was something in his face which made him look like
a schemer and he wished he had a little mirror to see. But there
could not be; and it was unjust and cruel and unfair.

He could not eat the blackish fish fritters they got on Wednesdays in lent and one of his potatoes had the mark of the spade in
it. Yes, he would do what the fellows had told him. He would go
up and tell the rector that he had been wrongly punished. A
thing like that had been done before by somebody in history, by
some great person whose head was in the books of history. And
the rector would declare that he had been wrongly punished because the senate and the Roman people always declared that the
men who did that had been wrongly punished. Those were the
great men whose names were in Richmal Magnall's Questions.
History was all about those men and what they did and that was
what Peter Parley's Tales about Greece and Rome were all about.
Peter Parley himself was on the first page in a picture. There was
a road over a heath with grass at the side and little bushes: and
Peter Parley had a broad hat like a protestant minister and a big
stick and he was walking fast along the road to Greece and Rome.

It was easy what he had to do. All he had to do was when the
dinner was over and he came out in his turn to go on walking

but not out to the corridor but up the staircase on the right that led to the castle. He had nothing to do but that: to turn to the right and walk fast up the staircase and in half a minute he would be in the low dark narrow corridor that led through the castle to the rector's room. And every fellow had said that it was unfair, even the fellow out of second of grammar who had said that about the senate and the Roman people.

What would happen?

He heard the fellows of the higher line stand up at the top of the refectory and heard their steps as they came down the matting: Paddy Rath and Jimmy Magee and the Spaniard and the Portuguese and the fifth was big Corrigan who was going to be flogged by Mr Gleeson. That was why the prefect of studies had called him a schemer and pandied him for nothing: and, straining his weak eyes, tired with the tears, he watched big Corrigan's broad shoulders and big hanging black head passing in the file. But he had done something and besides Mr Gleeson would not flog him hard: and he remembered how big Corrigan looked in the bath. He had skin the same colour as the turfcoloured bog-water in the shallow end of the bath and when he walked along the side his feet slapped loudly on the wet tiles and at every step his thighs shook a little because he was fat.

The refectory was half empty and the fellows were still passing out in file. He could go up the staircase because there was never a priest or a prefect outside the refectory door. But he could not go. The rector would side with the prefect of studies and think it was a schoolboy trick and then the prefect of studies would come in every day the same, only it would be worse because he would be dreadfully waxy at any fellow going up to the rector about him. The fellows had told him to go but they would not go themselves. They had forgotten all about it. No, it was best to forget all about it and perhaps the prefect of studies had only said he would come in. No, it was best to hide out of the way because when you were small and young you could often escape that way.

The fellows at his table stood up. He stood up and passed out among them in the file. He had to decide. He was coming near the door. If he went on with the fellows he could never go up to the rector because he could not leave the playground for that. And if he went and was pandied all the same all the fellows would

make fun and talk about young Dedalus going up to the rector
to tell on the prefect of studies.

He was walking down along the matting and he saw the door
before him. It was impossible: he could not. He thought of the
baldy head of the prefect of studies with the cruel nocoloured
eyes looking at him and he heard the voice of the prefect of studies
asking him twice what his name was. Why could he not remember
the name when he was told the first time? Was he not listening
the first time or was it to make fun out of the name? The great
men in the history had names like that and nobody made fun of
them. It was his own name that he should have made fun of if he
wanted to make fun. Dolan: it was like the name of a woman who
washed clothes.

He had reached the door and, turning quickly up to the right,
walked up the stairs and, before he could make up his mind to
come back, he had entered the low dark narrow corridor that led
to the castle. And as he crossed the threshold of the door of the
corridor he saw, without turning his head to look, that all the
fellows were looking after him as they went filing by.

He passed along the narrow dark carridor, passing little doors
that were the doors of the rooms of the community. He peered
in front of him and right and left through the gloom and thought
that those must be portraits. It was dark and silent and his eyes
were weak and tired with tears so that he could not see. But he
thought they were the portraits of the saints and great men of the
order who were looking down on him silently as he passed: saint
Ignatius Loyola holding an open book and pointing to the words
Ad Majorem Dei Gloriam in it; saint Francis Xavier pointing to
his chest; Lorenzo Ricci with his berretta on his head like one of
the prefects of the lines, the three patrons of holy youth – saint
Stanislaus Kostka, saint Aloysius Gonzago and Blessed John
Berchmans, all with young faces because they died when they
were young, and Father Peter Kenny sitting in a chair wrapped
in a big cloak.

He came out on the landing above the entrance hall and looked
about him. That was where Hamilton Rowan had passed and the
marks of the soldiers' slugs were there. And it was there that the
old servants had seen the ghost in the white cloak of a marshal.

An old servant was sweeping at the end of the landing. He
asked him where was the rector's room and the old servant

pointed to the door at the far end and looked after him as he went on to it and knocked.

There was no answer. He knocked again more loudly and his heart jumped when he heard a muffled voice say:

– Come in!

He turned the handle and opened the door and fumbled for the handle of the green baize door inside. He found it and pushed it open and went in.

He saw the rector sitting at a desk writing. There was a skull on the desk and a strange solemn smell in the room like the old leather of chairs.

His heart was beating fast on account of the solemn place he was in and the silence of the room: and he looked at the skull and at the rector's kindlooking face.

– Well, my little man, said the rector, what is it?

Stephen swallowed down the thing in his throat and said:

– I broke my glasses, sir.

The rector opened his mouth and said:

– O!

Then he smiled and said:

– Well, if we broke our glasses we must write home for a new pair.

– I wrote home, sir, said Stephen, and Father Arnall said I am not to study till they come.

– Quite right! said the rector.

Stephen swallowed down the thing again and tried to keep his legs and his voice from shaking.

– But, sir . . .

– Yes?

– Father Dolan came in today and pandied me because I was not writing my theme.

The rector looked at him in silence and he could feel the blood rising to his face and the tears about to rise to his eyes.

The rector said:

– Your name is Dedalus, isn't it?

– Yes, sir.

– And where did you break your glasses?

– On the cinderpath, sir. A fellow was coming out of the bicycle house and I fell and they got broken. I don't know the fellow's name.

The rector looked at him again in silence. Then he smiled and said:

– O, well, it was a mistake; I am sure Father Dolan did not know.

– But I told him I broke them, sir, and he pandied me.

– Did you tell him that you had written home for a new pair? the rector asked.

– No, sir.

– O well then, said the rector, Father Dolan did not understand. You can say that I excuse you from your lessons for a few days.

Stephen said quickly for fear his trembling would prevent him:

– Yes, sir, but Father Dolan said he will come in to-morrow to pandy me again for it.

– Very well, the rector said, it is a mistake and I shall speak to Father Dolan myself. Will that do now?

Stephen felt the tears wetting his eyes and murmured:

– O yes sir, thanks.

The rector held his hand across the side of the desk where the skull was and Stephen, placing his hand in it for a moment, felt a cool moist palm.

– Good day now, said the rector, withdrawing his hand and bowing.

– Good day, sir, said Stephen.

He bowed and walked quietly out of the room, closing the doors carefully and slowly.

But when he had passed the old servant on the landing and was again in the low narrow dark corridor he began to walk faster and faster. Faster and faster he hurried on through the gloom excitedly. He bumped his elbow against the door at the end and, hurrying down the staircase, walked quickly through the two corridors and out into the air.

He could hear the cries of the fellows on the playgrounds. He broke into a run and, running quicker and quicker, ran across the cinderpath and reached the third line playground, panting.

The fellows had seen him running. They closed round him in a ring, pushing one against another to hear.

– Tell us! Tell us!

– What did he say?

– Did you go in?

– What did he say?

– Tell us! Tell us!

He told them what he had said and what the rector had said and, when he had told them, all the fellows flung their caps spinning up into the air and cried:
– Hurroo!
They caught their caps and sent them up again spinning sky-high and cried again:
– Hurroo! Hurroo!
They made a cradle of their locked hands and hoisted him up among them and carried him along till he struggled to get free. And then he had escaped from them they broke away in all directions, flinging their caps again into the air and whistling as they went spinning up and crying:
– Hurroo!
And they gave three groans for Baldyhead Dolan and three cheers for Conmee and they said he was the decentest rector that was ever in Clongowes.
The cheers died away in the soft grey air. He was alone. He was happy and free; but he would not be anyway proud with Father Dolan. He would be very quiet and obedient: and he wished that he could do something kind for him to show him that he was not proud.
The air was soft and grey and mild and evening was coming. There was the smell of evening in the air, the smell of the fields in the country where they digged up turnips to peel them and eat them when they went out for a walk to Major Barton's, the smell there was in the little wood beyond the pavilion where the gall-nuts were.
The fellows were practising long shies and bowling lobs and slow twisters. In the soft grey silence he could hear the bump of the balls: and from here and from there through the quiet air the sound of the cricket bats: pick, pack, pock, puck: like drops of water in a fountain falling softly in the brimming bowl.

James Joyce (1882–1941), *A Portrait of the Artist as a Young Man*

6

ASSORTED STORIES

GET UP AND BAR THE DOOR

This old story was handed on by word of mouth before it was written down, about two hundred years ago.

There lived a man at the foot of a hill,
　John Blunt it was his name;
And he sold liquor and yill[1] of the best,
　Which earned him wondrous fame.

Now it fell about the Martinmas time
　(And a gay time it was then),
That Janet his wife did puddings make
　And boiled them in the pan.

The wind blew cold from north to south,
　It blew across the floor;
Quoth old John Blunt to Janet his wife:
　'Rise up and bar the door!'

'My hands are in my housewife keep,[2]
　Good man, as ye may see,
And if ye will not bar it yerself
　It will ne'er be barred by me.'

They make a paction[3] 'twict them twain,
　They made it firm and sure,
That the one that spake the foremost[4] word
　Was to rise and bar the door.

[1] ale　　　　　　　[2] busy with housework
[3] an agreement　　[4] first

183

Then by there came two gentlemen,
   Were riding over the moor;
And they came unto John Blunt's house
   Just by the light of the door.

'Now whether is this a rich man's house,
   Or whether is it a poor?'
But never a word spake man or wife
   For the barring of the door.

They came within and bad them good e'en,
   And then bade them good morrow;
But never a word spake man or wife,
   For the barring of the door, O.

O, first they ate the white pudding,
   And then they ate the black;
Though Janet thought muckle[5] to herself,
   Yet never a word she spake.

O, then they drank of the liquor so strong,
   And then they drank of the yill.
'O, now we have gotten a house of our own
   I'm sure we may take our fill.'

Then said one gentleman to his friend:
   'Here, man, take thou my knife,
Do thou scrape off this goodman's beard
   While I kiss his goodwife.'

'But there's no water in the house –
   How shall I shave him then?'
'What ails thee with the pudding bree[6]
   That boils within the pan?'

O, up then started old John Blunt,
   And an angry man was he:
'Will ye kiss my wife before mine eyes
   And scald me with pudding-bree?'

[5] much
[6] what's wrong with the water the pudding has been boiled in?

Then up and started Janet his wife,
    Gave three skips upon the floor:
'Goodman, ye've spoken the foremost word,
    Get up and bar the door!'

Ballad

A FAMOUS VICTORY

Gulliver's Travels, by Dean Swift, is one of the most-read books ever written. It tells of visits to countries where people are smaller or larger than usual, or hardly recognisable as human beings at all. The first voyage was to Lilliput, where Gulliver prevents an invasion of the country by the people of Blefuscu.

The Empire of Blefuscu is an island situated to the north-north-east side of Lilliput, from whence it is parted only by a channel of eight hundred yards wide. I had not yet seen it, and upon this notice of an intended invasion, I avoided appearing on that side of the coast, for fear of being discovered by some of the enemy's ships, who had received no intelligence of me, all intercourse between the two empires having been strictly forbidden during the war, upon pain of death, and an embargo laid by our Emperor upon all vessels whatsoever. I communicated to his Majesty a project I had formed of seizing the enemy's whole fleet: which, as our scouts assured us, lay at anchor in the harbour ready to sail with the first fair wind. I consulted the most experienced seamen, upon the depth of the channel, which they had often plumbed, who told me, that in the middle at high-water it was seventy *glumgluffs* deep, which is about six foot of European measure; and the rest of it fifty *glumgluffs* at most. I walked towards the north-east coast over against Blefuscu; and lying down behind a hillock, took out my small pocket perspective-glass, and viewed the enemy's fleet at anchor, consisting of about fifty men of war, and a great number of transports: I then came back to my house, and gave order (for which I had a warrant) for a great quantity of the strongest cable and bars of iron. The cable was about as thick as packthread, and the bars of the length and size of a knitting-needle. I trebled the cable to make it stronger, and for the same reason I twisted three of the iron bars together, binding the extremities into a hook. Having thus fixed fifty hooks to as many cables, I went back to the north-east coast, and putting off my coat, shoes, and stockings, walked into the sea in my leathern jerkin, about half an hour before high water. I waded with what haste I could, and swam in the middle about thirty yards till I felt ground; I arrived at the fleet in less than half an hour. The enemy was so frighted when they saw me, that they leaped out of their ships, and swam to shore, where there could not be fewer than thirty thousand souls. I then took my tackling, and fastening a hook to the hole at the prow of each, I tied all the cords together at the end. While I was thus employed, the enemy discharged several thousand arrows, many of which stuck in my hands and face; and besides the excessive smart, gave me much disturbance in my work. My greatest apprehension was for my eyes, which I should have infallibly lost, if I had not suddenly thought of an expedient. I kept among other little necessaries a pair of spectacles in a private pocket, which, as I observed before, had scaped the Emperor's searchers. These I took out and fastened as strongly as I could upon my nose, and thus armed went on boldly with my work in spite of the enemy's arrows, many of which struck against the glasses of my spectacles, but without any other effect, further than a little to discompose them. I had now fastened all the hooks, and taking the knot in my hand, began to pull; but not a ship would stir, for they were all too fast held by their anchors, so that the boldest part of my enterprise remained. I therefore let go the cord, and leaving the hooks fixed to the ships, I resolutely cut with my knife the cables that fastened the anchors, receiving above two hundred shots in my face and hands; then I took up the knotted end of the cables to which my hooks were tied, and with great ease drew fifty of the enemy's largest men-of-war after me.

The Blefuscudians, who had not the least imagination of what I intended, were at first confounded with astonishment. They had seen me cut the cables, and thought my design was only to let the ships run a-drift, or fall foul on each other: but when they perceived the whole fleet moving in order, and saw me pulling at the end, they set up such a scream of grief and despair, that it is almost impossible to describe or conceive. When I had got out of danger, I stopt awhile to pick out the arrows that stuck in my hands and face, and rubbed on some of the same ointment that was given me at my first arrival, as I have formerly mentioned. I then took off my spectacles, and waiting about an hour, till the tide was a little fallen, I waded through the middle with my cargo, and arrived safe at the royal port of Lilliput.

The Emperor and his whole court stood on the shore expecting the issue of this great adventure. They saw the ships move forward in a large half-moon, but could not discern me, who was up to my breast in water. When I advanced to the middle of the channel, they were yet in more pain, because I was under water to my neck. The Emperor concluded me to be drowned, and that the enemy's fleet was approaching in a hostile manner: but he was soon eased of his fears, for the channel growing shallower every step I made, I came in a short time within hearing, and holding up the end of the cable by which the fleet was fastened, I cried in a loud voice, *Long live the most puissant Emperor of Lilliput!* This great prince received me at my landing with all possible encomiums, and created me a *Nardac* upon the spot, which is the highest title of honour among them.

His Majesty desired I would take some other opportunity of bringing all the rest of his enemy's ships into his ports. And so unmeasurable is the ambition of princes, that he seemed to think of nothing less than reducing the whole empire of Blefuscu into a province, and governing it by a Viceroy; of destroying the Big-Endian exiles, and compelling that people to break the smaller end of their eggs, by which he would remain the sole monarch of the whole world. But I endeavoured to divert him from this design, by many arguments drawn from the topics of policy as well as justice; and I plainly protested, that I would never be an instrument of bringing a free and brave people into slavery. And when the matter was debated in council, the wisest part of the ministry were of my opinion.

This open bold declaration of mine was so opposite to the schemes and politics of his Imperial Majesty, that he could never forgive it; he mentioned it in a very artful manner at council, where I was told that some of the wisest appeared, at least by their silence, to be of my opinion; but others, who were my secret enemies, could not forbear some expressions, which by a side-wind reflected on me. And from this time began an intrigue between his Majesty and a junto of ministers maliciously bent against me, which broke out in less than two months, and had like to have ended in my utter destruction. Of so little weight are the greatest services to princes, when put into the balance with a refusal to gratify their passions.

Jonathan Swift (1667–1745), *Gulliver's Travels*

THE REAPING RACE

Liam O'Flaherty was born in the Aran Islands, off the west coast of Ireland. He writes plays and stories.

At dawn the reapers were already in the rye field. It was the big rectangular field owned by James McDara . . . McDara himself . . . was standing outside the fence on the sea-road, waving his stick and talking to a few people. . . .

'I measured it out yesterday,' he was saying, 'as even as it could be done . . . When I fire my revolver, they'll all start together and the first couple to finish their strip gets a five pound note. . . .'

The peasants were almost as excited as McDara himself, for the three best reapers in the whole island of Inverara had entered for the competition. They were now at the top of the field ready to begin. Each had his wife with him to tie the sheaves as they were cut and bring food and drink. . . .

On the left were Michael Gill and his wife Susan. Michael was a long wiry man with fair hair that came down over his forehead and was cropped to the bone all around the skull. . . . His lean jaws were continually moving backwards and forwards. . . .

In the middle Johnny Bodkin stood with his arms folded and his legs spread wide apart, talking to his wife in a low serious voice. He was a huge man, with fleshy limbs and neck, and black hair that had gone bald over his forehead . . .

On the right were Pat Considine and his wife Kate . . . Pat was a small man, small and slim and beginning to get wrinkles on his face although he was not yet forty. . . .

Then McDara waved his stick. He lifted his arm. A shot rang out. The reaping race began. In a moment the three men sank to their right knees like soldiers on parade at musketry practice . . . The curved reaping-hooks whirled in the air, and then there was a crunching sound, the sound that hungry cows make eating long fresh grass in spring. . . . The three women waited in ner-

vous silence for the first sheaf. It would be an omen of victory or
defeat. One, two, three, four bunches ... Johnny Bodkin, snort-
ing like a furious horse, was dropping his bunches almost without
stopping. With a loud cheer he raised his reaping hook in the air
and spat on it, crying, 'First sheaf!' His wife dived at it with
both hands and tied it ....

Working in the same furious manner in which he had begun,
Bodkin was soon far ahead of his competitors. He was cutting his
sheaves in an untidy manner and he was leaving hummocks
behind him on the ground owing to the irregularities of his
strokes, but his speed and strength were amazing. ...

Considine and his wife were second. Considine, now that he
was in action, showed surprising strength and an agility that was
goat-like. When his lean, long bony arms moved to slash the rye,
muscles sprang up all over his bent back like an intricate series
of springs being pressed. ...

Michael Gill and his wife came last. Gill had begun to reap
with the slow methodic movements of a machine driven at low
pressure. He continued at exactly the same pace, never changing,
never looking up to see where his opponents were. ...

As the day advanced people gathered from all quarters watching the reapers. The sun rose in the heavens. There was a fierce
heat. Not a breath of wind. ... Already there was a large irregular gash in the rye, ever increasing. ... Through the hum of
conversation the regular crunching of the reaping hooks could
be heard.

A little before noon Bodkin had cut half his strip. A stone had
been placed on the marking line at half-way, and when Bodkin
reached that stone, he stood up with the stone in his hand and
yelled: 'This is a proof,' he cried, 'that there was never a man
born in the island of Inverara as good as Johnny Bodkin.' ...
But big Kate Considine waved a sheaf above her head and yelled
in her rough man's voice, 'The day is young yet, Bodkin of the
soft flesh!' ...

Bodkin's wife was the first to go for the midday meal ... and
Bodkin began to eat and drink with as much speed as he had
reaped the rye. ... The Bodkin couple had no children, and on
that account they could afford to live well, at least far better
than the other peasants. Bodkin dropped his reaping-hook and
ravenously devoured three of the eggs, while his wife, no less

hungry, ate the fourth. . . . As soon as they had finished eating
they set to work again as fiercely as ever.

Considine had come level with Bodkin just as Bodkin resumed
work, and instead of taking a rest for their meal . . . Kate Considine fed her husband as he worked. . . . In that way he was
still almost level with Bodkin when he had finished eating. The
spectators were greatly excited at this eagerness on the part of
Considine, and some began to say that he would win the race.

Nobody took any notice of Gill and his wife, but they had
never stopped to eat, and they had steadily drawn nearer to their
opponents. They were still some distance in the rear, but they
seemed quite fresh, whereas Bodkin appeared to be getting
exhausted . . . and Considine was obviously using up the reserves
of his strength. Then, when they reached the stone at half-way,
Gill quietly laid down his hook and told his wife to bring the
meal. . . . They ate slowly, and then rested for a while. . . .
After about twenty minutes they got up to go to work again. . . .

Then, indeed, excitement rose to a high pitch because the Gill
couple resumed work at a great speed. . . . Now Bodkin's
supremacy was challenged. He was still a long way ahead of
Michael Gill, but he was visibly tired, and his hook made mistakes now and again, gripping the earth with its point. . . .

Just before four o'clock Pat Considine suddenly collapsed,
utterly exhausted. He had to be carried over the fence . . . He
made an effort to go back to work, but he was unable to rise. . . .

But all centred their attention on the struggle between Bodkin
and Gill. Spurred by rage, Bodkin had made a supreme effort,
and he began to gain ground once more. . . . But still, when he
paused at five o'clock to cast a look behind him, there was Gill
coming with terrible regularity. Bodkin suddenly felt all the
weariness of the day overcome him.

It struck him first in the shape of an intense thirst. He sent his
wife up to the fence for their extra can of tea. When she came
back with it he began to drink. But the more he drank the
thirstier he became. His friends in the crowd of spectators
shouted at him in warning, but his thirst maddened him. He
kept drinking. The shore-wall and victory were very near now.
He kept looking towards it in a dazed way as he whirled his hook.
And he kept drinking. Then his senses began to dull. He became
sleepy. His movements became almost unconscious. He only saw

the wall, and he fought on. He began to talk to himself. He
reached the wall at one end of his strip. He had only to cut down
to the other end and finish. Three sheaves more, and then . . .
Best man in Inverara . . . Five pound note . . .

But just then a ringing cheer came to his ears, and the cry rose
on the air: 'Gill has won!' Bodkin collapsed with a groan.

Liam O'Flaherty, *Short Stories*

THE MAN-EATER

It sometimes happens that, through thorns in their pads or injuries of various kinds, tigers are unable to catch the animals on which they normally prey. They then turn to eating men, and in the North of India little villages have suffered dreadful loss and lived in terror of the local man-eater. Jim Corbett became known as the man who could rid a district of its scourge. Here he is hunting a tiger which has stopped all work in the district, and caused the inhabitants of the largest village to abandon their homes and leave their land uncultivated.

I have told you of some of the attempts I made during this period of seven days and seven nights to get a shot at the tigress, but these were by no means the only attempts I made. I knew that I was being watched and followed, and every time I went through the two miles of jungle between my camp and Thak I tried every trick I have learnt in a lifetime spent in the jungles to outwit the tigress. Bitter though my disappointment was, I felt that my failure was not in any way due to anything I had done or left undone.

My men when they rejoined me said that, an hour after the kakar had barked, they had heard the tigress calling a long way off but were not sure of the direction. Quite evidently the tigress had as little interest in goats as she had in buffaloes, but even so it was unusual for her to have moved at that time of day from a locality in which she was thoroughly at home, unless she had been attracted away by some sound which neither I nor my men had heard; however that may have been, it was quite evident that she had gone, and as there was nothing further that I could do I set off on my weary tramp to camp.

The path, as I have already mentioned, joins the ridge that runs down to Chuka a quarter of a mile from Thak, and when I now got to this spot where the ridge is only a few feet wide and from where a view is obtained of the two great ravines that run

down to the Ladhya River, I heard the tigress call once and
again across the valley on my left. She was a little above and to
the left of Kumaya Chak, and a few hundred yards below the
Kot Kindri ridge on which the men working in that area had
built themselves grass shelters.

Here was an opportunity, admittedly forlorn and unquestion-
ably desperate, of getting a shot; still it was an opportunity and
the last I should ever have, and the question was, whether or not
I was justified in taking it.

When I got down from the tree I had one hour in which to
get back to camp before dark. Calling up the men, hearing what
they had to say, collecting the goats and walking to the ridge had
taken about thirty minutes, and judging from the position of the
sun which was now casting a red glow on the peaks of the Nepal
hills, I calculated I had roughly half an hour's daylight in hand.
This time factor, or perhaps it would be more correct to say
light factor, was all-important, for if I took the opportunity that
offered, on it would depend the lives of five men.

The tigress was a mile away and the intervening ground was
densely wooded, strewn over with great rocks and cut up by a
number of deep nullahs, but she could cover the distance well
within the half-hour – if she wanted to. The question I had to
decide was, whether or not I should try to call her up. If I called
and she heard me, and came while it was still daylight and gave
me a shot, all would be well; on the other hand, if she came and
did not give me a shot some of us would not reach camp, for we
had nearly two miles to go and the path the whole way ran
through heavy jungle, and was bordered in some places by big
rocks, and in others by dense brushwood. It was useless to con-
sult the men, for none of them had ever been in a jungle before
coming on this trip, so the decision would have to be mine. I
decided to try to call up the tigress.

Handing my rifle over to one of the men I waited until the
tigress called again and, cupping my hands round my mouth
and filling my lungs to their utmost limit, sent an answering call
over the valley. Back came her call and thereafter, for several
minutes, call answered call. She would come, had in fact already
started, and if she arrived while there was light to shoot by, all the
advantages would be on my side, for I had the selecting of the
ground on which it would best suit me to meet her. November

is the mating season for tigers and it was evident that for the past
forty-eight hours she had been rampaging through the jungles
in search of a mate, and that now, on hearing what she thought
was a tiger answering her mating call, she would lose no time in
joining him.

Four hundred yards down the ridge the path runs for fifty
yards across a flat bit of ground. At the far right-hand side of this
flat ground the path skirts a big rock and then drops steeply, and
continues in a series of hairpin bends, down to the next bench.
It was at this rock I decided to meet the tigress, and on my way
down to it I called several times to let her know I was changing
my position, and also to keep in touch with her.

I want you now to have a clear picture of the ground in your
mind, to enable you to follow the subsequent events. Imagine
then a rectangular piece of ground forty yards wide and eighty
yards long, ending in a more or less perpendicular rock face.
The path coming down from Thak runs on to this ground at its
short or south end, and after continuing down the centre for
twenty-five yards bends to the right and leaves the rectangle on
its long or east side. At the point where the path leaves the flat
ground there is a rock about four feet high. From a little beyond
where the path bends to the right, a ridge of rock, three or four
feet high, rises and extends to the north side of the rectangle,
where the ground falls away in a perpendicular rock face. On
the near or path side of this low ridge there is a dense line of
bushes approaching to within ten feet of the four-foot-high rock
I have mentioned. The rest of the rectangle is grown over with
trees, scattered bushes, and short grass.

It was my intention to lie on the path by the side of the rock
and shoot the tigress as she approached me, but when I tried this
position I found it would not be possible for me to see her until
she was within two or three yards, and further, that she could get
at me either round the rock or through the scattered bushes on
my left without my seeing her at all. Projecting out of the rock,
from the side opposite to that from which I expected the tigress
to approach, there was a narrow ledge. By sitting sideways I
found I could get a little of my bottom on the ledge, and by
putting my left hand flat on the top of the rounded rock and
stretching out my right leg to its full extent and touching the
ground with my toes, retain my position on it. The men and

goats I placed immediately behind, and ten to twelve feet below me.

The stage was now set for the reception of the tigress, who while these preparations were being made had approached to within three hundred yards. Sending out one final call to give her direction, I looked round to see if my men were all right.

The spectacle these men presented would under other circumstances have been ludicrous, but was here tragic. Sitting in a tight little circle with their knees drawn up and their heads together, with the goats burrowing in under them, they had that look of intense expectancy on their screwed-up features that one sees on the faces of spectators waiting to hear a big gun go off. From the time we had first heard the tigress from the ridge, neither the men nor the goats had made a sound, beyond one suppressed cough. They were probably by now frozen with fear – as well they might be – and even if they were, I take my hat off to those four men who had the courage to do what I, had I been in their shoes, would not have dreamt of doing. For seven days they had been hearing the most exaggerated and blood-curdling tales of this fearsome beast that had kept them awake the past two nights, and now, while darkness was coming on, and sitting unarmed in a position where they could see nothing, they were listening to the man-eater drawing nearer and nearer; greater courage, and greater faith, it is not possible to conceive.

The fact that I could not hold my rifle, a D.B.450/400 with my left hand (which I was using to retain my precarious seat on the ledge) was causing me some uneasiness, for apart from the fear of the rifle's slipping on the rounded top of the rock – I had folded my handkerchief and placed the rifle on it to try to prevent this – I did not know what would be the effect of the recoil of a high velocity rifle fired in this position. The rifle was pointing along the path, in which there was a hump, and it was my intention to fire into the tigress's face immediately it appeared over this hump, which was twenty feet from the rock.

The tigress however did not keep to the contour of the hill, which would have brought her out on the path a little beyond the hump, but crossed a deep ravine and came straight towards where she had heard my last call, at an angle which I can best describe as one o'clock. This manœuvre put the low ridge of rock,

over which I could not see, between us. She had located the
direction of my last call with great accuracy, but had misjudged
the distance, and not finding her prospective mate at the spot
she had expected him to be, she was now working herself up into
a perfect fury, and you will have some idea of what the fury of
a tigress in her condition can be when I tell you that not many
miles from my home a tigress on one occasion closed a public
road for a whole week, attacking everything that attempted to go
along it, including a string of camels, until she was finally joined
by a mate.

I know of no sound more liable to fret one's nerves than the
calling of an unseen tiger at close range. What effect this appalling
sound was having on my men I was frightened to think, and if
they had gone screaming down the hill I should not have been at
all surprised, for even though I had the heel of a good rifle to my
shoulder and the stock against my cheek I felt like screaming
myself.

But even more frightening than this continuous calling was
the fading out of the light. Another few seconds, ten or fifteen
at the most, and it would be too dark to see my sights, and we
should then be at the mercy of a man-eater, plus a tigress wanting
a mate. Something would have to be done, and done in a hurry,
if we were not to be massacred, and the only thing I could think
of was to call.

The tigress was now so close that I could hear the intake of
her breath each time before she called, and as she again filled
her lungs, I did the same with mine, and we called simultaneously. The effect was startlingly instantaneous. Without a
second's hesitation she came tramping with quick steps through
the dead leaves, over the low ridge and into the bushes a little to
my right front, and just as I was expecting her to walk right on
top of me she stopped, and the next moment the full blast of her
deep-throated call struck me in the face and would have carried
the hat off my head had I been wearing one. A second's pause,
then again quick steps; a glimpse of her as she passed between
two bushes, and then she stepped right out into the open, and,
looking into my face, stopped dead.

By great and unexpected good luck the half-dozen steps
the tigress took to her right front carried her almost to the exact
spot at which my rifle was pointing. Had she continued in the

direction in which she was coming before her last call, my story – if written – would have had a different ending, for it would have been as impossible to slew the rifle on the rounded top of the rock as it would have been to lift and fire it with one hand.

Owing to the nearness of the tigress, and the fading light, all that I could see of her was her head. My first bullet caught her under the right eye and the second, fired more by accident than with intent, took her in the throat and she came to rest with her nose against the rock. The recoil from the right barrel loosened my hold on the rock and knocked me off the ledge, and the recoil from the left barrel, fired while I was in the air, brought the rifle up in violent contact with my jaw and sent me heels over head right on top of the men and goats. Once again I take my hat off to those four men for, not knowing but what the tigress was going to land on them next, they caught me as I fell and saved me from injury and my rifle from being broken.

When I had freed myself from the tangle of human and goat legs I took the ·275 rifle from the man who was holding it, rammed a clip of cartridges into the magazine and sent a stream of five bullets singing over the valley and across the Sarda into Nepal. Two shots, to the thousands of men in the valley and in the surrounding villages who were anxiously listening for the sound of my rifle, might mean anything, but two shots followed by five more, spaced at regular intervals of five seconds, could only be interpreted as conveying one message, and that was, that the man-eater was dead.

I had not spoken to my men from the time we had first heard the tigress from the ridge. On my telling them now that she was dead and that there was no longer any reason for us to be afraid, they did not appear to be able to take in what I was saying, so I told them to go up and have a look while I found and lit a cigarette. Very cautiously they climbed up to the rock, but went no further for, as I have told you, the tigress was touching the other side of it. Late in camp that night, while sitting round a camp-fire and relating their experiences to relays of eager listeners, their narrative invariably ended up with, 'and then the tiger whose roaring had turned our livers into water hit the sahib on the head and knocked him down on top of us and if you don't believe us, go and look at his face.' A mirror is superfluous in camp and even if I had had one it could not have made the swelling on my jaw, which put me on milk diet for several days, look as large and as painful as it felt.

Jim Corbett (1875–1955), *The Man-eaters of Kumaon*

THE INVALID

Three Men in a Boat *was originally meant to be a serious book on the story of the River Thames. Somehow or other it turned into a comic account of a camping holiday taken by J. K. Jerome and his two friends. (Montmorency was the dog.) This is how the book starts; they then decide that they need a rest and a change in the shape of a holiday on the river.*

There were four of us – George, and William Samuel Harris, and myself, and Montmorency. We were sitting in my room, smoking, and talking about how bad we were – bad from a medical point of view I mean, of course.

We were all feeling seedy, and we were getting quite nervous about it. Harris said he felt such extraordinary fits of giddiness come over him at times, that he hardly knew what he was doing; and then George said that *he* had fits of giddiness too, and hardly knew what *he* was doing. With me, it was my liver that was out of order. I knew it was my liver that was out of order, because I had just been reading a patent liver-pill circular, in which were detailed the various symptoms by which a man could tell when his liver was out of order. I had them all.

It is a most extraordinary thing, but I never read a patent medicine advertisement without being impelled to the conclusion that I am suffering from the particular disease therein dealt with in its most virulent form. The diagnosis seems in every case to correspond exactly with all the sensations that I have ever felt.

I remember going to the British Museum one day to read up the treatment for some slight ailment of which I had a touch – hay fever, I fancy it was. I got down the book, and read all I came to read; and then, in an unthinking moment, I idly turned the leaves, and began to indolently study diseases, generally. I forget which was the first distemper I plunged into – some fearful, devastating scourge, I know – and, before I had glanced half down the list of 'premonitory symptoms,' it was borne in upon me that I had fairly got it.

I sat for a while frozen with horror; and then in the listlessness of despair, I again turned over the pages. I came to typhoid fever – read the symptoms – discovered that I had typhoid fever, must have had it for months without knowing it – wondered what else I had got; turned up St Vitus's Dance – found, as I expected, that I had that too – began to get interested in my case, and determined to sift it to the bottom, and so started alphabetically – read up ague, and learnt that I was sickening for it, and that the acute stage would commence in about another fortnight. Bright's disease, I was relieved to find, I had only in a modified form, and, so far as that was concerned, I might live for years. Cholera I had, with severe complications; and diphtheria I seemed to have been born with. I plodded conscientiously through the twenty-six letters, and the only malady I could conclude I had not got was housemaid's knee.

I felt rather hurt about this at first; it seemed somehow to be a sort of slight. Why hadn't I got housemaid's knee? Why this invidious reservation? After a while, however, less grasping feelings prevailed. I reflected that I had every other known malady in the pharmacology, and I grew less selfish, and determined to do without housemaid's knee. Gout, in its most malignant stage, it would appear had seized me without my being aware of it; and zymosis I had evidently been suffering with from boyhood. There were no more diseases after zymosis, so I concluded there was nothing else the matter with me.

I sat and pondered. I thought what an interesting case I must be from a medical point of view, what an acquisition I should be to a class. Students would have no need to 'walk the hospitals,' if they had me. I was a hospital in myself. All they need do would be to walk round me, and, after that, take their diploma.

Then I wondered how long I had to live. I tried to examine myself. I felt my pulse. I could not at first feel any pulse at all. Then, all of a sudden, it seemed to start off. I pulled out my watch and timed it. I made it a hundred and forty-seven to the minute. I tried to feel my heart. I could not feel my heart. It had stopped beating. I have since been induced to come to the opinion that it must have been there all the time, and must have been beating, but I cannot account for it. I patted myself all over my front, from what I call my waist up to my head, and I went a bit round each side, and a little way up the back. But I could not feel or hear anything. I tried to look at my tongue. I stuck it out as far as ever it would go, and I shut one eye, and tried to examine it with the other. I could only see the tip, and the only thing that I could gain from that was to feel more certain than before that I had scarlet fever.

I had walked into that reading-room a happy healthy man. I crawled out a decrepit wreck.

I went to my medical man. He is an old chum of mine, and feels my pulse, and looks at my tongue, and talks about the weather, all for nothing, when I fancy I'm ill; so I thought I would do him a good turn by going to him now. 'What a doctor wants,' I said, 'is practice. He shall have me. He will get more practice out of me than out of seventeen hundred of your ordinary, commonplace patients, with only one or two diseases each.' So I went straight up and saw him, and he said:

'Well, what's the matter with you?'

I said: 'I will not take up your time, dear boy, with telling you what is the matter with me. Life is brief, and you might pass away before I had finished. But I will tell you what is *not* the matter with me. I have not got housemaid's knee. Why I have not got housemaid's knee, I cannot tell you; but the fact remains that I have not got it. Everything else, however, I *have* got.'

And I told him how I came to discover it all.

Then he opened me and looked down me, and clutched hold of my wrist, and then he hit me over the chest when I wasn't expecting it – a cowardly thing to do, I call it – and immediately afterwards butted me with the side of his head. After that, he sat down and wrote out a prescription, and folded it up and gave it me, and I put it in my pocket and went out.

I did not open it. I took it to the nearest chemist's, and handed it in. The man read it, and then handed it back.

He said he didn't keep it.

I said: 'You are a chemist?'

He said: 'I am a chemist. If I was a co-operative stores and a family hotel combined, I might be able to oblige you. Being only a chemist hampers me.'

I read the prescription. It ran:

> '1 lb. beefsteak, with
> 1 pt. bitter beer
>   every 6 hours.
> 1 ten-mile walk every morning.
> 1 bed at 11 sharp every night.

And don't stuff up your head with things you don't understand.'

I followed the directions, with the happy result – speaking for myself – that my life was preserved, and is still going on.

Jerome K. Jerome (1859–1927), *Three Men in a Boat*

LOST AND FOUND

Gavin Maxwell acquired a rare kind of otter from the Tigris marshes, and took it to live with him in his lonely cottage in the West Highlands, where he led a Robinson Crusoe kind of life. Not far from the cottage a stream fell in waterfalls down a deep gorge.

Miji had early used his strength and resource to scale the Camusfeàrna waterfall and find out what lay beyond. Thereafter this inaccessible region had become his especial haunt, and one from which his extraction presented, even when he was not in difficulties, almost insuperable problems. The clamour of the falling water effectively drowned the calling human voice, and even if he did hear it there was little chance of the caller perceiving his faint, bird-like responses. On this occasion there was more water in the burn than is usual in summer, and there had been, too, a recent landslide, temporarily destroying the only practicable access from above. I lowered myself into the ravine on a rope belayed to the trunk of a tree, and I was wet to the waist after the first few yards of the burn's bed. I called and called, but my voice was diminished and lost in the sound of rushing water, and the little mocking birds answered me with Miji's own note of greeting. At length one of these birds, it seemed, called so repeatedly and insistently as to germinate in me a seed of doubt, but the sound came from far above me, and I was looking for Miji in the floor of the burn. Then I saw him; high up on the cliff, occupying so small a ledge that he could not even turn to make his way back, and with a fifty-foot sheer drop below him; he was looking at me, and, according to his lights, yelling his head off. I had to make a long detour to get above him with the rope and all the while I was terrified that the sight of me would have spurred him to some effort that would bring tragedy; terrified, too, that I myself might dislodge him as I tried to lift him from his eyrie. Then I found that the trees at the cliff-top were all rotten, and I had to make the rope fast to a stump on the

hill above, a stump that grew in soft peat and that gave out from
its roots an ominous squelching sound when I tugged hard on it.
I went down that rock with the rope knotted round my waist
and the feeling that Miji would probably survive somehow, but
that I should most certainly die. He tried to stand on his hind
legs when he saw me coming down above him, and more than
once I thought he had gone. I had put the loop of his lead
through the rope at my waist, and I clipped the other end to his
harness as soon as my arm could reach him, but the harnesses,
with their constant immersion, never lasted long, and I trusted
this one about as much as I trusted the stump to which my rope
was tied. I went up the rope with Miji dangling and bumping
at my side like a cow being loaded on to a ship by crane, and in
my mind's eye were two jostling, urgent images – the slow, sucking emergence of the tree roots above me, and the gradual parting
of the rivets that held Miji's harness together. All in all it was
one of the nastiest five minutes of my life; and when I reached
the top the roots of the stump were indeed showing – it took just
one tug with all my strength to pull them clean out.

But the harness had held, though, mercifully, it broke the next
time it was put to strain. Miji had been missing, that day in the
ravine, for nine hours, and had perhaps passed most of them on
that ledge, for he was ravenously hungry, and ate until I thought
he must choke.

There were other absences, other hours of anxiety and search,
but one in particular stands out in my mind, for it was the first
time that he had been away for a whole night, the first time that
I despaired of him. I had left him in the early morning at the
burn side eating his eels, and began to be uneasy when he had
not returned by mid-afternoon. I had been working hard at my
book; it was one of those rare days of authorship when everything seemed to go right; the words flowed unbidden from my
pen, and the time passed unheeded, so that it was a shock to
realize that I had been writing for some six hours. I went out and
called for Miji down the burn and along the beach, and when I
did not find him I went again to the ravine above the falls. But
there was no trace of him anywhere, though I explored the whole
dark length of it right to the high falls, which I knew that even
Miji could not pass. Just how short a distance my voice carried
I realized when, above the second falls, I came upon two wildcat

kittens at play on the steep bank; they saw me and were gone in
a flash, but they had never heard my voice above the sound of
the water. I left the burn then and went out to the nearer islands;
it was low tide, and there were exposed stretches and bars of soft
white sand. Here I found otter footprints leading towards the
lighthouse island, but I could not be certain that they were
Miji's. Later that summer his claws became worn so that his pad-
marks no longer showed the nails, but at that stage I was still
unsure of distinguishing his tracks from those of a wild otter,
unless the imprints were very precise. All that evening I searched
and called, and when dusk came and he still did not return I
began to despair, for his domestic life had led him to strictly
diurnal habits, and by sundown he was always asleep in front
of the fire.

It was a cloudy night with a freshening wind and a big moon
that swam muzzily through black rags of vapour. By eleven
o'clock it was blowing strong to gale from the south, and on the
windward side of the islands there was a heavy sea beginning to
pile up; enough, I thought, for him to lose his bearings if he were
trying to make his way homeward through it. I put a light in each
window of the house, left the doors open, and dozed fitfully in
front of the kitchen fire. By three o'clock in the morning there
was the first faint paling of dawn, and I went out to get the boat,
for by now I had somehow convinced myself that Miji was on
the lighthouse island. That little cockleshell was in difficulties
from the moment I launched her; I had open water and a beam
sea to cross before I could reach the lee of the islands, and she
was taking a slosh of water over her gunwale all the way. If I
shipped oars to bale I made so much leeway that I was nearly
ashore again before I had done, and after half an hour I was both
wet and scared. The bigger islands gave some shelter from the
south wind, but in the passages between them the north-running
sea was about as much as the little boat would stand, and over
the many rocks the skerries the water was foaming white and
wicked-looking in the half light. A moment to bale and I would
have been swept on to these black cusps and molars; the boats
would have been crunched on them like a squashed matchbox,
and I, who cannot swim a stroke, would have been feeding the
lobsters. To complete my discomfort, I met a Killer whale. In
order to keep clear of the reefs I had rowed well north of the

small islands that lie to landward of the lighthouse; the water was calmer here, and I did not have to fight to keep the nose of the boat into the waves. The Killer broke the surface no more than twenty yards to the north of me, a big bull whose sabre fin seemed to tower a man's height out of the water; and, probably by chance, he turned straight for me. My nerves were strung and tensed, and I was in no frame of mind to assess the true likelihood of danger; I swung and rowed for the nearest island as though man were a Killer's only prey. I grounded on a reef a hundred yards from the tern island, and I was not going to wait for the tide to lift me. Slithering and floundering in thigh-deep water over a rock ledge I struggled until I had lifted the flat keel clear of the tooth on which it had grated; the Killer, possibly intent upon his own business and with no thought for me, cruised round a stone's throw away. I reached the tern island, and the birds rose screaming around me in a dancing canopy of ghostly wings, and I sat down on the rock in the dim windy dawn and felt as desolate as an abandoned child.

The lighthouse island was smothered in its jungle-growth of summer briars that grip the clothing with octopus arms and leave trails of blood-drops across hands and face; on it I felt like a dream walker who never moves, and my calling voice was swept away northwards on gusts of cold, wet wind. I got back to the house at nine in the morning, with a dead-weight boat more than half full of water and a sick emptiness in my mind and body. By now part of me was sure that Miji too had met the Killer, and that he was at this moment half digested in the whale's belly.

All that day until four o'clock in the afternoon I wandered and called, and with every hour grew the realization of how much that strange animal companion had come to signify to me. I resented it, resent my dependence upon this subhuman presence and companionship, resented the void that his absence was going to leave at Camusfeàrna. It was in this mood, one of reassertion of human independence, that about five in the evening I began to remove the remaining evidence of his past existence. I had taken from beneath the kitchen table his drinking bowl, had returned for the half-full bowl of rice and egg, had carried this to the scullery, what the Scots call the back kitchen, and was about to empty it into the slop pail, when I thought I heard Miji's voice from the kitchen behind me. I was, however, very tired, and distrustful of my reactions; what I thought I had heard was the harshly whispered 'Hah' with which he was accustomed to interrogate a seemingly empty room. The impression was strong enough for me to set down the bowl and hurry back into the kitchen. There was nothing there. I walked to the door and called his name, but all was as it had been before. I was on my way back to the scullery when I stopped dead. There on the kitchen floor, where I had been about to step, was a large, wet footprint. I looked at it, and I thought: I am very tired and very overwrought; and I went down on my hands and knees to inspect it. It was certainly wet, and it smelled of otter. I was still in a quadrupedal attitude when from the doorway behind me I heard the sound again, this time past mistaking – 'Hah.' Then Miji was all over me, drenched and wildly demonstrative squeaking, bouncing round me like an excitable puppy, clambering on my shoulders, squirming on his back, leaping, dancing. I had been reassuring myself and him for some minutes before I realized that his harness was burst apart, and that for many hours, perhaps a day or more, he must have been caught like Absalom, struggling, desperate, waiting for a rescue that never came.

Gavin Maxwell (1914–   ), *Ring of Bright Water*

ACKNOWLEDGMENTS

Thanks are due to Mr R. J. Harris for suggesting two passages, and to the following authors, or their representatives, for permission to include copyright material: R. K. Gordon and J. M. Dent and Sons Ltd., *Anglo-Saxon Poetry*; J. H. Williams and Rupert Hart-Davis Ltd., *Elephant Bill*; the Estate of the late Mrs Frieda Lawrence and Laurence Pollinger Ltd., *Phoenix*; Gerald Durrell and Rupert Hart-Davis Ltd., *The Bafut Beagles*; Angus Graham and A. D. Peters and Co., *The Golden Grindstone*; Maurice Hussey and Heinemann Educational Books, *The Chester Mystery Plays*; C. S. Lewis and The Bodley Head, *Out of the Silent Planet*; M. V. Hughes and the Oxford University Press, *A London Family Chronicle*; Gwen Raverat and Faber and Faber Ltd., *Period Piece*; Sir Arthur Grimble and John Murray Ltd., *Pattern of Islands*; F. H. Burnett and William Heinemann Ltd., *The Secret Garden*; John Masefield and Wells Gardner, Darton and Co. Ltd., *Jim Davis*; James Thurber Copyright © 1963 Hamish Hamilton Ltd., *Vintage Thurber*; Raymond Williams and Chatto and Windus Ltd., *Border Country*; the Executors of the James Joyce Estate and Jonathan Cape Ltd., *A Portrait of the Artist as a Young Man*; Liam O'Flaherty and Jonathan Cape Ltd., *The Short Stories of Liam O'Flaherty*; Jim Corbett and the Oxford University Press, *Man-Eaters of Kumaon*; Jerome K. Jerome and J. M. Dent and Sons Ltd., *Three Men in a Boat*; and Gavin Maxwell and Longmans Green and Co. Ltd., *Ring of Bright Water*.